Susan Audap
510-~~577-1077~~
510-434-9394

❖ HOW CAN I FIX IT?
Finding Solutions
and
Managin

D0461914

HOW CAN I FIX IT?
Finding Solutions and Managing Dilemmas

An Educator's Road Map

LARRY CUBAN

Teachers College, Columbia University
New York and London

Copyright © 2001 by Teachers College, Columbia University

All rights reserved. No part of this publication may be reproduced or transmitted in any form or by any means, electronic or mechanical, including photocopy, or any information storage and retrieval system, without permission from the publisher.

Library of Congress Cataloging-in-Publication Data

Cuban, Larry.
   How can I fix it? : Finding solutions and managing dilemmas : An educator's road map / Larry Cuban.
      p.   cm.
   Includes bibliographical references (p.).
   ISBN 0-8077-4049-7 (pbk. : alk. paper)
    1. School management and organization—Handbooks, manuals, etc.
   2. Problem solving—Handbooks, manuals, etc.   I. Title.
   LB3011 .C886 2001
   371.2—dc21   00-054494

ISBN 0-8077-4049-7

Printed on acid-free paper
Manufactured in the United States of America
08   07   06   05   04   03   02   01   8   7   6   5   4   3   2   1

For Sondra and Janice,
who have taught me so much about
solving problems and managing dilemmas

Contents ❖

Acknowledgments ❖

I have been lucky in my career. I have been both a practitioner and a professor. For a quarter-century beginning in 1955, I taught social studies in big city schools (14 years) and served as an administrator (11 years, 7 of which were as a school superintendent). As a practitioner I had plenty of problems, dilemmas, and changes to juggle.

When I became a professor in 1981, for the first time I had time to reflect on my practitioner experiences. I researched puzzling questions about the history of teaching and school reform. I also read texts and firsthand accounts of folks who sought to improve their problem-solving skills. To keep my memories of teaching and administering fresh, I taught a high-school social-studies class for a semester on three different occasions. I also served as an associate dean for two years.

In 1985, I began to offer workshops on solving problems locally to practitioners in our Stanford/Schools Collaborative and in the Bush Educators program in Minnesota. The materials that I initially used were drawn from my school experiences and case studies. Over the past 15 years, workshop participants have critiqued my approaches, suggested alternative methods, and told of their experiences in classrooms, schools, and districts. I have listened to their criticisms, kept changing the presentations, and compiled their accounts. It is from these experiences that I have woven this *Practitioner's Guide*.

First, I want to thank those many workshop participants for their blunt and friendly critiques. I also thank John Mauriel, former director and designer of the best professional-development experience in the nation, for inviting me in 1985 to be a faculty member of the Bush Educators program (1975–2000) that worked with Minnesota superintendents, principals, and teachers. For the support and encouragement of Carole Saltz, Director of Teachers College Press, who over the years has found a home for many of my books, I am most appreciative. Finally, I thank the Center for Advanced Studies in the Behavioral Sciences for the fellowship (1999–2000) that permitted me to complete writing on several projects, including this book, while enjoying the company of a bunch of superb Fellows.

Introduction ❖

This *Guide* to solving problems and managing dilemmas is practitioner-driven. The concepts, language, examples, and cases are crafted intentionally to appeal to an audience of teachers and administrators who are deeply interested in improving how they solve problems and manage dilemmas in classrooms, schools, and districts. I offer concepts and skills that have worked for other practitioners and for me over the years.

Let me be clear on one point. I do not fool myself into believing that reading this *Guide* will produce the knowledge, skills, and attitudes necessary to solve problems and manage dilemmas expertly. I can, for example, describe the physical principles behind bicycle riding, but these principles are no substitute for the practical knowledge and skills that come into play from actually riding a bike. Some veteran bicyclists can run alongside rookie riders and coach them on how to turn the wheels one way or lean another way, and on what to look for as they manage to pump pedals, steer, and move in the right direction. When veteran bikers are learning how to do speed trials or are climbing mountains, coaches ride alongside the novices (experienced as they may be in other bicycling venues) to share their expertise.

No book—not even this one—can claim that one will be an expert problem solver as a result of reading it. But if readers take situations they have experienced in classrooms, schools, and districts and apply the suggestions in the book, the chances increase of putting into practice what is offered here.

Part I of the book lays out how I approach the framing of problems and dilemmas. In Part I, I concentrate on the importance of defining what the problem is (rather than designing the solution), then distinguish between routine problems and messy dilemmas. I offer many examples of these concepts. For many of the examples I detail a step-by-step analysis elaborating and illustrating the concepts of framing problems and dilemmas. A selection of actual and composite cases with accompanying questions follows the conceptual portion for readers to apply what they have learned. There is an Appendix in which I offer my answers to the questions accompanying the cases.

Part II is about the links between problems and dilemmas and planned changes. In this section, I distinguish between incremental and fundamental changes in schools and how each kind of change is viewed as a solution to a problem or a compromise to a dilemma. As in Part I, I end the section with a few cases that illustrate different kinds of problems and the changes that have been introduced in the form of solutions.

Thus, this *Guide* offers "riding alongside the bicycle" help to those who want to learn more about framing problems, managing dilemmas, and negotiating changes. The cases and examples described here give readers a chance to apply their knowledge and skills to their situations. No book, including this one, however, will convert a reader into an expert problem solver or dilemma manager. What I can promise is that there will be many chances for readers to apply what has been written here in both their personal and professional lives.

I have enjoyed thoroughly the past 15 years of holding workshops for and with practitioners on framing problems and dilemmas as well as figuring out changes that address those situations. What follow are the collected experiences, reflections, and cases contained in a *Guide* for practitioners who share my passion for understanding better how we approach the complexities of teaching, learning, and schooling.

PART I

Framing Problems and Dilemmas

If there is one task that practitioners pride themselves on, it is solving problems. Teachers face classroom situations daily in which routine and non-routine conflicts occur; similarly, principals wrestle with school issues that call for negotiating differences calmly and making changes in attitudes, behaviors, and procedures. In mastering the craft of teaching and principaling, practitioners become expert problem solvers. They see a situation, size it up swiftly, figure out what has to be done, and then do it. Another problem solved! Handling problems becomes second nature to experienced practitioners.

Because the process is so familiar, expert teachers and principals often have difficulty explaining to novices what it is that they do to solve problems. Much like a veteran teacher trying to tell a rookie how she can detect an inattentive student in the back of the classroom in a flash, without any noises occurring, exact words are hard to find. In this guide for practitioners, I look closely at the process of solving problems and inspect those parts that often go unexamined to offer readers a way to think about messy situations and a common vocabulary for framing and solving problems. Because we live in a can-do culture, the result, the solution, the outcome is far more important than how the problem was initially defined. Too often, solutions are mismatched to the problem or simply botched when applied because so little time was spent on determining what the problem really was. I believe it is a serious error to concentrate more on solutions than on figuring out what the problem is. Knowing about the process of

framing or defining a problem—I use the phrases interchangeably—
is essential for each of us in becoming more aware of how we actually
solve rather than botch problems.

❖ WHAT IS A PROBLEM?

A common answer to the question is that a problem is a situation in which a gap is found between what *is* and what *ought to be*. To
close the gap, obstacles must be overcome. There are, for example, 32 students in the class, and the teacher has only 24 textbooks. Why is the
teacher 8 books short? Two other teachers have taken all the other copies
for their classes. The teacher's goal is for each student to have a book.
There is a gap between what is and what ought to be. He has to figure
out a workable solution to his problem with the other teachers and the
32 students. The teacher has identified a problem to be solved.[1]

Two parents have written letters (with copies to the superintendent)
complaining about an experienced and popular middle-school social-
studies teacher who has taught lessons on the pros and cons of abortion.
The parents are upset, each for opposite reasons, about the films, speak-
ers, and text materials that the teacher has used in the class to present
both sides of the controversial issue.

One parent's goal is to encourage the teacher to do more on the subject; the other parent's goal is to prevent the teacher from dealing with
this controversial topic. The principal's goals are to protect the teacher
from intrusions in the classroom, respond fairly and swiftly to parents
on both sides of the abortion issue, and have the superintendent see
that she is doing her job well. There is a large gap between what is
(parental complaints about the teacher) and what ought to be (the parents', teacher's, and principal's different goals). She has identified a problem with several obstacles blocking solutions.

These two problems were discovered by those directly involved in the
situation. Framing a problem, then, is a subjective process.

Defining a problem depends on the perceptions of the person or
group that interprets facts showing a discrepancy between what *is* and
what *ought to be*. What shape our perceptions are the previous personal
and work experiences that we have had, our beliefs and values, and the
position that we have in an organization (and the roles that we are
expected to play in that position). What appears as a problem to the

teacher in the first example may not be viewed as a problem, for example, by the two other teachers who got to the storeroom before the one who came up short on texts. Neither may the bookless students view the situation as a problem. In short, in any given situation, there is no objective or true definition of a problem. How a problem is framed depends on who is doing the defining.

Framing a problem also involves conflict and power. If defining a problem is subjective, there will always be individuals and groups who differ as to whether there is a problem and what qualifies as a good solution. Influence and authority determine whose subjective view of what is a problem becomes the dominant one. The social-studies teacher who believes that it is his academic freedom to teach about abortion does not see his decision as a problem. The principal, sensitive to the community implications of parents' complaints about a volatile social issue (and the superintendent's perceptions of her job performance), has the power to determine that this, indeed, is a problem. Subjectivity, conflict, and power are features inherent in identifying and framing situations as problems.

❖ THE PROBLEM-SOLVING PROCESS

The process of solving problems is often described as a series of steps that have to be followed, one after the other. Figure 1 lays out a linear sequence of stages. Within these stages, I have combined three processes.

- ◆ Problem solving
- ◆ Decision making
- ◆ Changing

To solve problems, an individual or group must take some initiative—even risk—by first identifying the problem, framing it, generating solutions, deciding on a solution, and taking action that alters what routinely occurs in order to solve the problem. Moving through these various steps involves solutions' becoming planned changes that have to be implemented.[2]

The three processes of problem solving, decision making, and change are deeply entangled. (I will elaborate on the processes of problem

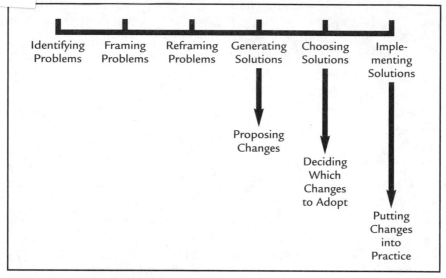

FIGURE 1. Problem Solving and the Change Process

solving and decision making later in Part I and on the process of change in Part II.) As a result, it is possible that expert problem solvers will fall flat on their faces when they tackle problems, because the processes of decision making and changing each have their own complexities, apart from the intricacies of framing and solving problems.

Of course, because framing and solving problems is subjective and involves power and conflict, it is hardly linear. It is circular and episodic, and it follows a hip-hop course more often than each of us would like to remember. Sometimes steps are skipped; at other times, steps are repeated again and again. That is what Figure 2 illustrates.

The most common pattern for practitioners who view themselves as experts in solving problems is to identify a problem selectively (that's where the subjectivity enters) by providing some factual evidence that a gap exists between what is and ought to be. They then leap to a favorite solution for situations similar to the current one. That has been my experience as a teacher, trainer of teachers, superintendent, and professor. Each of us carries in our heads a repertoire of solutions that fit situations we frame as problems. When the cues from the situation in front of us ring bells, out comes a solution that we have used in similar settings.

Pavlov

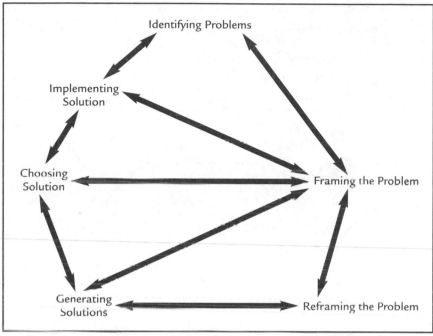

FIGURE 2. Problem Solving in Practice

This spontaneous reaction should come as no surprise, because practitioners are action-driven professionals who must make instant decisions in classroom and school situations. A teacher, for example, defines a student who is perennially tardy as a problem. Sure enough, the student arrives tardy for the fourth time—one more time than the three each student is permitted. In the few seconds that it takes for the student to enter and sit at her desk, the teacher has shifted into the problem-solving mode with a solution that has worked in the past with tardy students. Similarly, a principal faced with a new instructional policy that he knows will annoy his teachers if he executes it as mandated by the central office defines the new policy as a problem to be solved and has at his fingertips favored ways of dealing with distasteful district policies.

Leaping from quickly defining the problem to a solution that seems to fit the problem is understandable for busy practitioners who often lack the time to consider other options fully or reflect on how they framed the problem initially. Although the quick-time decisions are understandable, they may be counterproductive, especially if swiftly decided solutions carry consequences and may lead to undesirable outcomes that have to be addressed later. Based on the many times that I have had to remedy bad solutions that I had grafted on to poorly defined problems, I have concluded that for certain situations—particularly those that have high stakes attached to them—taking time to frame what the problem is and considering alternative solutions carefully actually *saves* time. Or as one teacher put it: "Why is it we never have the time to do it right but time to do it over?"

Others also have seen that how we state the problem is crucial to determining which solutions we pursue. Albert Einstein did not hesitate to say, "The formulation of a problem is often more essential than its solution." The careful framing of a problem is the essential first step in moving down the road to solutions. Hence, most of what follows will focus on framing problems and the common traps awaiting practitioners rather than on determining which solutions are best.[3]

❖ FRAMING A PROBLEM: THE BLAME TRAP

Pointing the finger of blame at individuals, groups, or institutions makes it easier for those who frame the problem to concentrate on one target for a solution. If whoever is to blame changes, the problem will be solved. *Voila!* The danger, of course, is that a blame-filled statement of a problem may exclude possible causes of an undesirable situation other than the targeted person or group.

For example, a high-school history teacher goes to the new assistant principal and says that two youths have been disrupting the class continually since the semester began by talking in class, not doing their assigned reading in class, and in general ignoring the teacher's directions. The teacher wants the two students transferred immediately. The new assistant principal accepts the teacher's way of framing the problem as a student problem (that is, the two students are causing the trouble because they continually and willfully disobey the teacher) and transfers the two students to another history class.

A month later, the same teacher appears in the assistant principal's office asking that two more students be removed for causing disturbances in the class. The assistant principal asks the teacher why two more students should be transferred, and the teacher reports the same disrespectful and disobedient acts that the previous students had committed.

But this time, instead of removing another two students, the administrator decides to gain more information. She checks to see how the other students whom she had transferred are doing in their new class and finds that the other teacher is satisfied with both their academic work and their behavior. The assistant principal then examines the previous year's record of referrals from the teacher, the academic records of the students who have been placed in that history teacher's class, and the teaching evaluations of the teacher's classroom practices. She considers the teacher's role in creating a situation in which students misbehave. (Is this an inexperienced teacher? Does the teacher use the same method of teaching day in and day out?) The assistant principal also seeks specific information about the teacher's classes. (What is the range of students' different abilities, performance, and ethnicity in each of the classes?) The administrator is trying to figure out another way to define the problem, one that is fault-free: What is happening in this classroom that creates an unhealthy situation for both students and teacher? In framing the situation this way, she avoids finding fault in the students or the teacher; she considers other factors, as well.

No-fault framing becomes an essential ingredient in stating problems that leave open a more generous range of alternatives to explore for a solution. A fault-free definition becomes especially important for the ill-defined problems that most teachers and principals face in their daily work.

❖ TAME AND WICKED PROBLEMS (A.K.A. DILEMMAS)

Tame problems are the familiar, routine, and frequent situations that practitioners face. For teachers and administrators, these problems often involve procedures (e.g., giving a test to a class you are convinced will copy from one another, too much classroom time taken in collecting lunch money); malfunctioning equipment (e.g., bulbs that blow out in the overhead projector); and managing relationships (e.g., conflict between two teachers in the same grade over what is to be covered in the year's curriculum). As common as tame problems are, they still need to be solved. Experienced practitioners have a large repertoire of solutions that fit particular routine problems. In most districts, policy manuals lay out step-by-step ways to deal with routine problems.

Tame problems, however, are not central to this guide for practitioners. Wicked problems are.[4]

Wicked problems are ill-defined, ambiguous, complicated, interconnected situations packed with potential conflict. In organizations, wicked problems arise when people compete for limited resources (e.g., we cannot fund both the new phonics program and smaller class size for K–3; we will have to choose); hold conflicting values (e.g., the time that I usually spend preparing for my classes and reading students' essays is preventing me from spending time with my family and earning enough money to make mortgage and car payments); and wrestle with diverse expectations held by others about what practitioners should be doing (e.g., principals are supposed to be instructional leaders, competent managers, astute politicians, and skilled therapists). These complicated, entangled situations produce conflict within each practitioner, among practitioners, within the organization, and among organizations. Unlike tame problems, wicked problems cannot be solved. Although wicked problems can be managed, they cannot be solved. They are insoluble. Calling wicked problems "problems," then, is a misnomer. "Wicked problems" are really dilemmas.

Dilemmas are messy, complicated, and conflict-filled situations that require undesirable choices between competing, highly prized values that cannot be simultaneously or fully satisfied. Most teenagers, for example, often face the same dilemma: how to rebel and conform at the same time. Many figure out a way to reconcile both values by defying their parents and copying one another.

A common situation facing teachers is deciding which grade to assign to a graduating high-school senior who comes to class on time, completes homework regularly, asks to do extra credit, is quiet in class, is polite in exchanges with the teacher and classmates, but fails more than half the quizzes and exams during the year. The teacher has to choose between passing or failing the student. What makes this situation a dilemma and not a tame problem?

The teacher is torn by competing values and has to make unpleasant choices. The teacher personally values hard work, determination, and motivation. Further, as a professional she wants to uphold the standards of the subject in which she teaches and believes. Also, the organization that pays her salary wants her to uphold the district's academic standards in assigning grades. Yet the teacher knows that passing and failing the student each will have adverse and positive consequences for the student. Passing the student means a diploma, celebrations, and no more school. Failing the student means no graduation or diploma now and going to summer school.

Even passing the student contains negative lessons: being quiet and polite are more important than competency in a subject; having a diploma falsely advertises to employers and professors that the student has the requisite knowledge and skills to perform. The high-stakes conflict causes the teacher pain, yet a decision must be made and recorded on a report card.

Or consider a common dilemma faced by a principal in a district where the policy is for school-site administrators to spend at least one day a week observing teachers and writing a monthly report to district headquarters on what has been observed in classrooms. The principal, once a teacher himself, knows that what teachers want from a principal is not weekly oversight in their classrooms. They want a school that runs smoothly with administrative support in dealing with angry parents and disobedient students. What makes this situation a dilemma and not another tame problem?

The principal is conflicted. He values being a loyal subordinate in the district's chain of command. He is expected to execute district policy. Someday he may even want an administrative job in the district office. But the principal, as a former teacher, also values teachers' classroom autonomy and respects their professionalism. He knows that some faculty members will view weekly visits and his taking notes in the back of the room as threatening because he also evaluates each teacher in the school.

These values clash. How, then, can the principal finesse these conflicting values? What choices does he have? Should he make perfunctory visits of a few minutes each, take no notes, reassure the teachers that all is well, and write a bland report? Or should he do what the policy mandates and report to his superiors the results of his weekly visits? Or should he consult with teachers about the policy and jointly determine what would advance the school's goals best in complying with this policy? The uncertainty accompanying the consequences of each choice underscores the ambiguity inherent in coping with dilemmas.

These examples of dilemmas common to practitioners are built into the complex roles teachers and administrators play in schools and districts. Although individuals bring different personal values to their jobs, powerful organizational values such as efficiency, equity, and effectiveness intersect with these personal values to create conflicts.

From the outside, these dilemmas look like tame problems because of the gap between what is and what ought to be. They even feel like tame problems (some degree of conflict is common to both), but they are far messier, less structured, and often intractable to routine solutions. They become dilemmas rather than tame problems when organizational constraints make it impossible for any prized value to triumph. Every person, every organization operates under constraints of time, money, laws, cultural and political assumptions, and other conditions that limit what can be done at any one point in time. Unattractive decisions (often based on inadequate information) must be made in the face of these conditions to secure as many of the competing, prized values as possible. These choices often become compromises, ways to reconcile conflicting and highly desirable options.[5]

Unlike tame problems—there may be tried and tested ways to collect lunch money or complete a form evaluating a teacher—dilemmas are rarely addressable using technical solutions. There are no "smart" bombs for dilemmas. There are only ambiguous, uncertain, and jerry-built compromises that last for a while.

Dilemmas, then, end up with good-enough compromises, not neat solutions. As Herbert Simon says, we "satisfice" when we cope with dilemmas. That is, in order to satisfy, we must sacrifice. We construct a tightrope to walk between competing claims, knowing that crossing the tightrope juggling the competing values will still leave us uneasy, or even tense. We negotiate the unappealing choices within dilemmas by tying contraries together in some fashion to cope with different but sought-after values. Moreover, these good-enough bargains among values that we strike have to be renegotiated again and again, because circumstances and people change. Thus, more often than not, we end up managing recurring dilemmas, not solving problems. The key features of a dilemma are as follows.[6]

- ◆ Competing prized values
- ◆ Unattractive choices due to constraints
- ◆ Satisficing (compromising)
- ◆ Managing, not solving

Analyzing a Dilemma

Consider how the experiences of Mrs. Dorothy Ramirez, a new teacher, touch on each of these features. In a culturally diverse high school with 1,300 students in northern California, Ramirez teaches 10th grade biology. In one of her five classes she has 32 students, of whom one-third are Latino, one-third are African American, and one-third are white. Alberto, a 17-year-old Latino who has turned in his assignments on time and hovers between a C and D in academic performance, has begun disrupting the class.[7]

Recently, Alberto has begun to talk with those around him while the teacher or other students are engaged in lectures or whole-group discussions. Even after Ramirez quietly and persistently asks Alberto to stop, he continues these side conversations. On two occasions, Ramirez keeps Alberto after class for a few minutes to ask whether there is something awry in school or class to account for his behavior. He says nothing. The next day, he repeats the behavior during another student's presentation and is rude to Ramirez when she asks him to stop. Two other students also begin smirking and talking to each other while the teacher listens to students give their opinions during a whole-group discussion. Ramirez asks Alberto to leave class for 10 minutes to cool off outside the door, and he does. The same thing happens the following day.

Ramirez decides to call home, because she fears that she is losing control of Alberto. If this occurs, it might spread like an infection to the rest of the class. She calls his parents and discovers that they speak only Spanish. Because she speaks only English, Ramirez enlists the help of a Spanish-speaking counselor at school, who calls Alberto's home and speaks with his mother. The mother tells the counselor that she, too, is having trouble with Alberto, the oldest of her three children, and she promises to speak to him.

The next day in biology class, Alberto has another run-in with Ramirez over the same conduct. The teacher calls the counselor and mother, and they meet the following day. In the meeting, the teacher and counselor learn that the mother can't control Alberto at home. Ramirez suggests speaking with the father. The mother gets very upset, because the father works two jobs to support the family, and if he finds out about Alberto's behavior at school and home, he will beat the boy, as he has before. The meeting adjourns with no action taken but deep concern over what to do if Alberto causes more trouble in class.

Ramirez has the following options before her:

♦ Keep Alberto out of class for another 10-minute time-out until he settles down.

◆ Refer Alberto to the assistant principal and recommend a three-day
   suspension for constant disruptiveness in class. Such a suspension
   will trigger a meeting with both parents prior to Alberto's return to
   school.
◆ Send Alberto to an in-school suspension class for five days, where a
   security monitor makes sure that students work on their homework
   and behave. No meeting with parents will be required.

Ramirez has reached the bottom of her bag of techniques in dealing with
disruptive students. Nothing seems to work. She now faces a dilemma
in which a choice needs to be made. Yet each choice has decided pluses
and minuses for the teacher, Alberto, and the rest of the class. Entangled
in the choices are conflicting values that make each bittersweet.

Ramirez values the class's right to learn without interference from a
disruptive student; yet she prizes helping an individual student whose
behavior has become puzzlingly disruptive. She likes very much bringing parents into school to help alleviate a difficult situation, but not at
the cost of causing harm to the student. She searches for the option that
best satisfices or reconciles the conflicts. She knows that the trade-offs
accompanying satisficing will leave her dissatisfied, but some compromise must be constructed, because Alberto's actions in her biology class
are creating an untenable situation. She also knows that the option she
chooses may fail, and that she will then have to find other compromises
to cope with Alberto. There is no question in Ramirez's mind that she is
dealing not with a tame problem but a hard-core dilemma.

Is the Distinction Between Tame Problems
and Dilemmas Useful?

Distinguishing between tame problems and dilemmas is hardly
original. Philosophers and social scientists have made the point often.
Moreover, lawyers and judges are thoroughly familiar with the notion of
balancing competing claims and seeking compromises that will satisfy
adversaries. Economists routinely deal with trade-offs among values in
making decisions, and politicians clearly understand the language of
bargaining and logrolling.

A skeptic, however, could question the conceptual distinction that I
make on the grounds that just because other professionals are familiar

with it, and just because I find it both useful and compelling, it still may not be credible with practitioners. For such skeptics, here are a few reasons that I believe a focus on dilemmas rather than tame problems is worthwhile for teachers and administrators.[8]

First, at the heart of educational practice is decision making. All practitioners at one time or another must act. To act, they must choose. Invariably, the choices involve competing moral values. For example, when half of the students in a class copies from one another during a major test, a teacher has to choose among ignoring the cheating (strengthening the value of harmony in the class but weakening the value of honesty), picking out one of the cheaters and making an example of the person (honoring the values of honesty and courage but undermining the value of fair treatment), or confronting all of those who have cheated and taking some action (the values of honesty, decisiveness, fairness, and courage).

Or consider a situation in which the district office has directed all principals to implement a new kindergarten promotion policy that calls for retaining for another year all students who score below the 60th percentile on a standardized test. The principal and the majority of the faculty in a school in which 75 percent of the African American students are receiving government-subsidized free lunches are dead-set against the policy. They have been convinced by their experiences with children that low-achieving kindergartners will catch up in skills and knowledge if given time. Moreover, they know the research findings on the negative academic and social effects of retaining 5-year-olds. They oppose such a policy because they believe it will harm their young children. Professional values of making independent judgments about what is correct and incorrect practice about their students conflicts with the value of loyalty to the organization that pays their salaries. It is now the end of May, and 25 percent of the kindergartners have scored below the 60th percentile. Decisions about promotion and retention must be made in two weeks. Whether to oppose the policy openly, construct an option that creates a special class, merge K–1 grades into one unit, or implement the district's policy are options that the teachers consider. Making choices, often moral ones, then, is central to practice.

Another reason for concentrating on dilemmas is that Americans think of problems as just waiting to be solved in a can-do spirit. "Pragmatic Americans," wrote Luigi Barzini, "consider the very existence of problems intolerable and life with problems unacceptable. They believe

... that all problems not only must be solved, but also that they can be solved, and that in fact the main purpose of a man's life is the solution of problems." One British observer called Americans: " 'Godsakers.' For God's sake do something!" American culture prizes getting the job done, using speedy and efficient technology, and asking the basic question: Will it work? Acknowledging that many situations are intractable and require managing through negotiating trade-offs goes against the cultural grain and creates guilt over failing to remedy problems. Americans have a hard time with the idea of intractable or insoluble problems.[9]

This is why a distinction between problems and dilemmas can be helpful. In a can-do culture, a pervasive cloud of guilt hangs over practitioners who face recurring, messy situations and repeatedly fail to "solve" the "problem." Repeated failures of highly touted solutions leave a debris of disappointment—even cynicism—among well-intentioned educators. Distinguishing between problems that can be solved and dilemmas that require satisficing can reduce guilt. We can pursue ways to frame those dilemmas to get unstuck from familiar "solutions" and create better compromises.

Explicit analysis of these inevitable predicaments may also lead to more imaginative definitions of dilemmas. For example, Gunnar Myrdal's study of U.S. race relations in the 1930s and its history went beyond the customary definition of racial troubles as a "Negro Problem." Myrdal, a Swedish social scientist, saw that the beliefs in equality, the land of opportunity, and freedom—what he called the American Creed—conflicted with Jim Crow practices and the second-class social status that blacks had endured in America. To Myrdal, the situation was no longer a Negro Problem but a clash of choices within white Americans' souls between social and economic advantages gained from segregation and the historic ideals of equality and freedom. It was an American Dilemma.[10]

In framing a historic problem as a dilemma, Myrdal helped moved the traditional debate from how best to uplift the Negro economically to how to arouse white Americans from their moral slumber over the gap between democratic beliefs and racist behavior. This intellectual definition of the situation, of course, became the basis for the moral authority of the Civil Rights Movement in the 1950s and 1960s and its leaders' extraordinary success in reducing the distance between Americans' ideals and racial practices, a struggle that continues today.

The intractability of the national and historic issue of race may overwhelm readers. Turn to the mundane situation faced by Phyllis Reed at Larchmont High School.

The Case of the Disappointed High-School Department Head

Phyllis Reed completed her first year as chair of the Larchmont High School social-studies department without distinction. She still felt like an outsider. Her efforts to establish rapport had succeeded only with Susan Smith, the other female department member, and the two newest additions to the department. The other eight department members continued to resent the fact that the principal, Horace Jones, had gone to another school in the district to hire a 35-year-old woman, instead of giving the job to Tom Yarney, a 20-year veteran scholar and revered advanced-placement (AP) American government teacher who had applied for the position in response to pressure from his colleagues in the department.[11]

Reed replaced a conscientious teacher, Steve Jones, who had chaired the department for seven years before retiring. He had been selected because no one else wanted to put up with the administrative details and required school meetings. Jones had done a satisfactory job of managing the department's books and supplies but used his one free period (instead of teaching five classes, Jones, as department chair, taught only four) to work on his class preparation rather than exercise departmental leadership. The decision to select an outsider was part of the principal's long-term goal of promoting more active student learning. Although the social-studies department was not the easiest starting place, he thought it was generally respected on campus. He knew that Reed was an outstanding teacher and thought she could use her skills as a designer of cooperative learning activities and a teacher of writing to transform classrooms in the department and ultimately influence schoolwide practices.

As a group, the teachers in the department strongly valued their privacy and believed it was everyone's right to teach without interference. Most teachers emphasized the importance of mastering basic knowledge in their subject areas, which they genuinely loved. Susan Smith made regular use of imaginative assignments in her AP American history classes and was trying to organize her 9th grade world geography units around central questions. Bob, a third-year teacher, made extensive use of group work and simulations in world history and had organized a small model United Nations club. And John, a veteran teacher, focused heavily on the use of writing as a tool for learning in his government and U.S. history classes, even using student portfolios.

Reed and the principal observed that the teachers enjoyed talking together in the faculty lunchroom or after school, but that they talked about sports or the lack of administrative follow-through on discipline and attendance problems rather than about the curriculum, teaching, and learning.

In her classroom visits, Reed observed that most teachers lectured and led question–answer "discussions" for the first part of the period, then supervised an early start of homework to stress learning of important knowledge and minimize student disruptions. She was pleased that the teachers were enthusiastic about their subjects, but was alarmed that they were becoming increasingly frustrated with students' lack of interest.

Student attendance, effort, and achievement were admirable in the AP courses, but only about 12 percent of the student body enrolled in these classes. Average daily attendance in non-AP social-studies classes had dropped from 80 percent to 69 percent during the previous two years (about consistent with the rest of the school). According to the teachers, the overwhelming majority of students lacked interest in learning; were unwilling to do assigned work; and were unable to pass tests, even when the questions were reviewed ahead of time in detail. The percentage of students outside of honors classes receiving grades of D or F had increased from 34 percent to 42 percent during the previous academic year.

Larchmont has experienced major demographic changes. Ten years earlier, the school was 85 percent white. The present population is approximately 50 percent white, 35 percent Latino, 7 percent black, and 8 percent Asian American. The non-white population is projected to grow by 6 percent next year.

Because the teachers normally stayed in their classrooms working at their desks, Reed's primary contact with department members came when they stopped in her office, a large converted classroom, to pick up supplies. One-half of the office was partitioned into a supply room, with four rows of floor-to-ceiling shelves displaying titles of book and pamphlets going back 25 years. The other half was a cluttered but open area containing her desk, a six-foot work table, a ditto machine, and six metal four-drawer file cabinets holding old department records, worksheets, exams, and mimeograph stencils.

Reed had hoped to promote changes by leading valuable monthly department meetings and being an effective supervisor of instruction. She worked especially hard designing meetings on grades, cooperative learning activities, and the new state social-studies framework. In one department meeting focusing on the increase in Ds and Fs, eight of the 12 teachers, all veterans, argued vigorously that the low grades stemmed from students' irresponsibility and that standards should be maintained. They argued that they had a moral obligation to teach the current students the same effective way that they had been teaching since the school had opened in 1965.

After the department meeting, in which Reed distributed copies of her best lesson plans, illustrating how she challenged all levels of students to use critical thinking skills in world history, one especially disgruntled teacher commented: "Where does she get off thinking she can tell us how to teach?"

Three teachers responded to Reed's offer of help to anyone interested in trying out one or more of her teaching ideas. Bob tried one cooperative learning activity suggested by Reed but became disillusioned when the noise got out of control and the teacher next door called on the intercom to complain. Susan Smith observed Reed working with small groups, but told her that the fast pace of AP work made cooperative learning a luxury she could not afford. Reed worked with the third volunteer, a beginning teacher, but classroom discipline problems made this a painful experience for both of them.

In the department meeting on the new state social-studies framework, teachers came without having read the document and argued with spirited humor bordering on pride that they had not taken these documents seriously in 15 years and saw no need to change now.

Reed had originally believed that her role as a supervisor of instruction could help her push gently for change. Most of her veteran staff (averaging 14 years of teaching experience), however, viewed supervision and evaluation as unnecessary. They felt uncomfortable during her full-period classroom visits and tried to make the follow-up discussions as perfunctory as possible, within the limits of civility. They all knew they were good teachers; the former chair had always written positive evaluations after his ten-minute class visits. He had known they were high-quality professionals who had better things to do than discuss and fill out forms for the district office.

What's her charge?

Reed was anxious as she headed for her end-of-the-year evaluation conference with Horace Jones. She knew that the principal was disappointed. There had been no change. Most teachers continued to teach primarily by providing information in well-organized lectures, as they had been taught in school and college. Reed saw little hope for improvement. Teaching assignments for the following year, which are based on seniority and academic specialty, would be the same; the teachers' attitudes would be the same; and no one was retiring or going on leave.

Questions

Here are some questions that probe your understanding of routine problems and dilemmas. After jotting down your answers, turn to Appendix A and see how I analyzed the case and answered the same questions. Keep in mind that framing problems and dilemmas is highly subjective, depending a great deal on one's experiences, values, and position or status held at the time. So there is no correct answer. But some answers are better than others. What distinguishes stronger from weaker answers is the quality of the reasoning and evidence that goes into the answer.

1. Is this a routine problem or a dilemma? Explain your answer.
2. According to Reed, what is the problem that has to be solved? Explain your reasoning. Evidence?
3. What would you guess Tom, Steve, John, or any of the other veteran teachers in the department would say is the primary problem that has to be solved? Explain your reasoning. Evidence?
4. What would you guess the principal would say is the primary problem that has to be solved? Explain your reasoning. Evidence?
5. If you decided that this was a routine problem, how would you frame it? If you decided that it was a dilemma, how would you frame it?

❖ HOW TO ANALYZE SITUATIONS IN FRAMING PROBLEMS AND DILEMMAS

The following advice is offered not as a blueprint or rules to follow but as a set of guidelines to consider. If the "how" of framing problems and dilemmas is subjective and varies considerably because of the influence and authority of those doing the defining, then guidelines to help negotiate a subjective terrain may be helpful. Moreover, the process appears as steps to follow on the printed page, but anyone familiar with trying to solve tame problems or manage dilemmas in his or her personal or professional life knows from experience that the process is seldom linear. More often, it zigzags.

With these cautions, I offer these guidelines drawn from my experiences and those of others who have tried to make sense of the complex processes of framing problems and dilemmas that are taken for granted in our daily lives. For some readers, these guidelines may seem cumbersome, too much to do in too short a time. If you are among such a group, I urge you to figure out shorthand ways that fit your experience, workplace, and style of learning. The central point to these guidelines is to identify the relevant values in a situation, know what values are important to you in your setting, analyze what already exists in the situation, and then define the problem or dilemma.[12]

1. *Identify the personal, professional, organizational, and societal values in the situation.*

Determining whether a situation is a routine problem or dilemma is the first step in dealing with problems and dilemmas. If the situation is defined as a routine problem, then tapping the arsenal of familiar solutions follows. If the problem is solved, no further analysis is necessary.

But if the problem recurs again and again, then reassessing the situation—particularly, figuring out which highly prized values are clashing—is necessary, because what has appeared initially as a tame problem is probably hiding a dilemma. What values are evident in the situation? Which ones compete for attention? To identify the values, a working definition and examples might help.

Basically, a "value" is an enduring and desirable belief that we have about something (an idea, a quality, an action, and a means of getting a task done). Freedom; efficient use of resources; fair treatment; fulfilling one's obligations to a friend, parent, or country; respect for differences; and logical thinking are examples of different values. Every goal that a person seeks or that an organization prizes has buried in it a value. If I internalize a value, it becomes a standard for guiding my actions and thoughts and for judging morally what others, and I, do. Value judgments ("What a terrible thing the school board did in giving teachers no pay raise," "Wasn't that wonderful what she did for the neighborhood?") are opinions based on internalized beliefs about what are desirable and undesirable actions. Table 1 lists examples of values. Consult the list, but do not confine yourself to it, because the list itself is incomplete. Add values that you see are missing from the list.

   2. *Identify the current compromises or ways to satisfice the situation.*

When values compete and choices must be made, satisficing occurs. What is the current compromise of acceptable trade-offs that has either unraveled or is being scrutinized? Which data are no longer relevant? What values are being reasserted (and by whom) that weaken the current compromise? When these questions are answered, a history of the reconciliation that has been worked out emerges, as do the reconciliation's weaknesses and its critics.

   3. *If the situation is one that you are analyzing but are uninvolved in,*
      list and rank the values, based on available data, in order of
      desirability from the point of view of the participants. If the situation
      is one in which you are directly involved, list and rank your values.

Yes, ranking values is highly subjective. You interpret evidence of what others prize and decide what to rank. Or you ask yourself: What do I prize most, second, third, etc.? This task occurs prior to and during constructing and negotiating the trade-offs that go into an acceptable compromise.

   4. *After identifying and ranking the relevant values in the situation,*
      reframe the situation to accommodate the ranked values in order
      to create a new compromise.

To begin reframing, which is an act of imagination and creativity, begin by asking: How was the situation originally framed? What were the key assumptions that went into the original framing of the dilemma? Which values were ranked the highest?

❖ REFRAMING PROBLEMS AND DILEMMAS

Probably the hardest task for practitioners to perform, individually or in groups, when they face a problem or dilemma is taking the time to think about reframing the situation in at least one way that is

TABLE 1. Illustrations of Values and Statements Representing Different Values

Categories of values	Illustrative statements
1. BASIC HUMAN VALUES	
Freedom	"I would not force teachers to chaperone the students' dance."
Happiness	"I'm pleased that most of the students feel good about it."
Respect for others	"If we put ethnic food in the lunchroom, the kids from other groups will enjoy it and understand why we did it."
Survival	"This is a job-security issue. We have to do something about it."
2. SOCIAL AND POLITICAL VALUES	
Fairness	"Make sure that those who are unsure of themselves have a chance to speak."
Courage	"I have the duty to speak out about the vandalism, even if it damages my friendship with people I have known for years."
Individualism	"I want to do this myself."
Helping	"Let's see if we can get Janice and Sondra to help Barbara work that out."
Participation	"We need to get the parents, teachers, and students involved in solving the attendance problem."
Loyalty	"We have to stick together on this issue."
3. PROFESSIONAL VALUES	
Autonomy	"I have the knowledge, skills, and training to handle this problem."
Obligation to organization	"That's what the policy says, and I have to carry it out."
Obligation to clients	"I have to do this because it is best for kids."
Power/control	"How can we achieve the goal if we cannot even determine how to spend the money?"
4. ORGANIZATIONAL VALUES	
Efficiency	"How can we get more bang out of each dollar we spend?"
Effectiveness	"Have we reached the targets we set for ourselves this year?"
5. PERSONAL VALUES	
Religious	"My beliefs in God help me through each day."
Ethnic/racial/gender	"The culture I grew up in is one that I want to make sure my children pass on to their children."

Source: Adapted from Kenneth Leithwood and Roseanne Steinbach, *Expert Problem Solving* (Albany, NY: State University of New York Press, 1995), p. 180.

different from the original definition. Reframing involves inventing new ways to interpret familiar situations. You have already read about instances of reframing. Recall the earlier example of the assistant principal trying to avoid blaming the teacher or students; also note the example of how Myrdal reframed the "Negro Problem" into the "American Dilemma."

Reframing is hard to do because practitioners are driven to act now, not later. It is hard to do because teachers and administrators get so used to looking at situations in habitual ways that stepping back to view the current situation from another angle takes not only an act of will but a repertoire of other ways of seeing the world. It is hard to do because there is no guarantee that the reframing—which, just like framing, is subjective and contingent on influence and authority—will lead to a better trade-off. A practitioner can reasonably ask: If I have to take the time, energy, and even risk to reflect and it won't necessarily yield a better outcome, why should I do it?

Indeed, why reframe? For high-stakes problems and dilemmas in which consequences matter a great deal for students, practitioners, parents, or the community, taking the time to reframe a situation offers the chance to generate different alternatives to solve a problem or negotiate a compromise that may have been absent from the original framing. We acknowledge the importance of reframing in everyday language. How many times have we heard the cliché: Don't see it as a problem, see it as an opportunity? An accreditation visit to a school can be seen as an incredible burden that has to be endured by already overworked administrators and teachers or a splendid chance for the faculty to come to grips with the changing demographics of their student body and show the district office and school board what this hardworking staff has really accomplished over the past five years. This is reframing the familiar. The imaginative reconceptualizing of the commonplace occurs often.

Reframing can be seen in the long history of the mechanical tomato picker. In the early years of the machine, the metal picking arms did extensive damage to the tomatoes, reducing profits. The problem was initially framed as: How can we improve the machine to inflict less damage in picking the fruit? The machines did get better at picking, but losses still ran high. Not until others reframed the problem from an engineering perspective (How can we improve the machine?) to a genetic one (How can we produce a tomato with a thicker rind that won't be easily damaged?) did profits begin to flow to agricultural businesses. The rest is history.[13]

Reframing can be seen in the shift in educators' thinking that has occurred over students' academic performance. As recently as the 1980s, the dominant belief among educators was that poor academic achievement, as measured by test scores, was due either to the effects of students' socioeconomic and cultural backgrounds or a lack of motivation on the part of individual students. In short, the problem of low test scores was framed as a student or family problem.

With the accelerating interest in "Effective Schools" research and the evidence of students in schools located in low-income minority areas performing above expectations, the problem of low test scores has been reframed since the 1990s as a school problem. Low faculty expectations, inappropriate instruction, an anti-academic climate, and a non-challenging curriculum bear as much responsibility as, if not more responsibility than, students' backgrounds for low academic performance. Schools are now expected to improve academic achievement far more than they were in previous decades.[14]

Finally, reframing can be seen in Mark Twain's *Tom Sawyer*. Tom is told that he has to whitewash 30 yards of a nine-foot-high board fence, and it is a Saturday afternoon when all of his friends are playing. As he paints, his friend Ben walks toward him, and Tom has an inspiration:

> "Hello, old chap, you got to work, hey?"
> "Why, it's you, Ben! I warn't noticing."
> "Say—I'm going a-swimming, I am. Don't you wish you could?"
> "But, of course you'd druther work—wouldn't you? Course you would!"

Tom contemplated the boy a bit and said:

> "What do you call work?"
> "Why ain't *that* work?"

Tom resumed his whitewashing and answered carelessly.

> "Well, maybe it is and maybe it ain't. All I know is, it suits Tom Sawyer."
> "Oh, come now, you don't mean to let on that you *like* it?"

The brush continued to move.

> "Like it? Well, I don't see why I oughtn't to like it. Does a boy get a chance to whitewash a fence every day?"

That put things in a new light. Ben stopped nibbling his apple. Tom swept his brush daintily back and forth—stepped back to note the effect—added a touch here and there—criticized the effect again—Ben watching every move and getting more and more interested, more and more absorbed.

Presently he said:

> "Say, Tom, let *me* whitewash a little.[15]

By the late afternoon, the fence has three coats of paint, and one boy after another has paid Tom for the privilege of painting a part of the fence. Tom has reframed work, even tedious work, into a pleasure that has a price.

In the cases of the mechanical tomato picker, "Effective Schools," and Tom Sawyer, individuals and small groups had invented imaginative ways to reframe situations within organizations, between and among organizations, and in one-to-one relationships. Quite often the people who develop skills in redefining familiar situations have in their heads more than one way of seeing the world. They have developed their capacity to juggle diverse ways of viewing daily occurrences. To the degree that one can hold in his or her mind multiple ways to see a situation, to that degree opportunities to reframe a problem and dilemma multiply.

Tools for reframing, different ways of seeing the world, can be found in using various perspectives drawn from different academic disciplines. Table 2 lays out four ways to see problems and dilemmas by specifying the assumptions to each perspective, the key questions that are implied in each viewpoint, and the change strategies that accompany each way of seeing.[16]

Now return to Phyllis Reed, our Larchmont High School social-studies chair who is so disappointed in what has happened in her first year leading the department. Using the four perspectives in Table 2, identify which of the ways of seeing that you initially used to define the problem or dilemma. Then reframe the problem or dilemma from at least one other of the viewpoints outlined in the table. If you want to see how I reframed the situation, turn to Appendix B.

TABLE 2. Ways of Viewing Problems and Dilemmas: Tools for Reframing

Psychological	Organizational	Political	Cultural
PREMISES			
Individuals' values, attitudes, traits, and background cause problems.	Situations and settings cause problems.	The uses of power and authority with individuals and groups cause problems.	Norms, rituals, expectations, and beliefs shape behavior; conflicting norms, etc., cause problems.
QUESTIONS IMPLIED IN WAY OF VIEWING			
Which personal values, background, and traits influence behavior?	Which features of the setting shape person's behavior?	Who gets what, for which purposes, when, and under what conditions?	What are the dominant formal and informal norms, beliefs, and rituals in the organization? In the sub-unit?
How can these be changed?	How can parts of a setting or an entire setting be changed?	Which people have the power to make changes?	How can parts of the culture be changed?
CHANGE STRATEGIES			
Alter person's beliefs and behavior through professional development, remediation, etc.	Modify goals, structures, roles, processes, etc., in the setting.	Alter the dominant coalition in the organization by building a new power base.	Make existing norms and expectations, beliefs, and ceremonies explicit; introduce new norms, language, and rituals and persist in reinforcing them.
	Redesign parts of the whole organization.		Improve skills of bargaining and conflict resolution.

❖ COMMON QUESTIONS THAT ARISE WHEN PRACTITIONERS BEGIN REFRAMING PROBLEMS AND DILEMMAS

After 15 years of teaching teachers, administrators, school-board members, and graduate students about problems and dilemmas, certain questions come up again and again. Here are three that practitioners frequently ask.

1. *If you see dilemmas where others see problems, does that mean you end up working less actively to improve a situation because dilemmas are insoluble?*

Seeing dilemmas does mean that you accept the view that certain situations are intractable within schools and classrooms (e.g., enduring tensions between centralizing and decentralizing administrative functions; negative socioeconomic effects of poverty on children coming to school). As insoluble as these situations may be, there are two reasons that unflagging efforts are needed to construct better compromises than currently exist. First, figuring out better ways to cope with dilemmas and reconciling the conflicting values better than they have been are professional responsibilities of practitioners. Second, small improvements in an intractable situation can make significant differences in children's lives. Qualified teachers and smaller high schools for low-income children, for example, are hardly solutions to unsatisfactory academic performance. They are improved compromises. Such incremental measures can make potent differences in what happens between teachers and students while reducing the impact of an enduring dilemma in urban schooling. Framing and reframing situations as dilemmas to find improved compromises requires, if anything, a great deal of imagination, energy, and initiative, not passivity.

2. *Can problems be wrapped in dilemmas?*

Yes. Because of the subjective nature of defining problems and dilemmas, where some see problems others see dilemmas. Similarly, there will be occasions when a dilemma contains—for you—tame problems.

Consider, for example, the following situation. At a Parent–Teachers Organization (PTO) meeting in January, two teachers (of a middle-school staff of 40) expressed their frustration with unruly students in the school's halls and a lack of administrative support in dealing with students who disrupted classes. The next day, the president of the PTO put a notice in all teachers' boxes identifying "school discipline" as an issue in need of immediate attention. The following week, the PTO newsletter that went to all parents of middle-school students contained a "call for action on student discipline" and included the minutes of the previous meeting.[17]

The president of the PTO asked the principal whether she and the vice-president could attend the next staff meeting to discuss with the faculty the issue of student discipline. The principal denied the request but offered to meet with the PTO officers. At that meeting, the principal and PTO representatives shared information and agreed that the last faculty meeting of the year would be an open forum on school discipline. At the June faculty meeting, comments from teachers were mixed. Half of the staff agreed that discipline was an issue, and half disagreed. During the summer, at the PTO's invitation, another meeting was held that 20 parents and 10 teachers attended. By the end of this meeting, it was clear that school discipline had been identified as a problem needing attention from both teachers and administrators.

In analyzing this situation, I see problems wrapped in a larger dilemma. First, it is unclear from the description of the situation that an actual problem exists in managing students' behavior at the middle school. Two teachers (out of 40 on staff) offered their opinions, drawn from their experiences about what was occurring in the school. Those opinions, amplified by the concerns of PTO officers, came to the attention of the principal and the entire staff. After a meeting with the principal, an open forum at the June faculty meeting, and a summer meeting for parents and teachers who wanted to come, school discipline was explicitly framed as a problem.

Yet no data had been presented on teachers' referrals of students to the assistant principal, suspensions from school, and other incidents from current and previous years. The subjective impressions of some parents and teachers had snowballed into a strong schoolwide belief in deteriorating discipline, without benefit of actual figures. There may well be a problem with school discipline, but without any statistics comparing current and past records within the school, or comparing the school with other middle schools in the district, it is hard to say. The problem is now one of perceptions that school discipline is a problem.

A principal and faculty can deal with this as a problem by collecting, analyzing, and communicating to the parents and staff of the school actual data on numbers of students getting into trouble in school. If the data support the perception of the problem, then the administration and staff can discuss why the problem has arisen, generate solutions,

choose the solutions that best fit the problem and school, and implement the favored solutions.

Yet the problem of perceptions unsupported by data reveals a larger
dilemma: the weak relationship between the principal and PTO officers
and the conflicting values of two different organizations (a parent-
dominated one and an administrator-dominated one). Each has a con-
stituency to whom it must respond; each has values embedded in its
organizational charter. Usually these organizations find common
ground and reconcile the conflicting values. Not in this case, however.

3. *Can you treat a dilemma as a problem and deal with it in bits and
   pieces?*

The above example of the PTO, school discipline, and staff of a middle school suggests that the answer is yes. I would, for example, urge the
principal to treat the situation initially as a perceptual problem and collect previous and current data to present to the staff and PTO. If the data
support the perceptions of an erosion in school discipline, then the
principal can deal with it at two levels: as a problem that has causes
located in varied factors, such as changing enrollments, teacher turnover,
lack of knowledge among students about school rules, and other pos-
sibilities. Each of these factors (individually and in combination with
one another) suggests alternative ways to frame the problem. Framing
the problem would then follow from an analysis of the data and inter-
views with teachers and students. Also, simultaneously, the principal
could treat the perceptual issues as a signal of a deep-seated dilemma
that needs a far better reconciliation of conflicting values than has
existed.

Another example of treating a dilemma as a problem in bits and
pieces is when elementary-school children come from homes where they
are taught to defend themselves when other students hit them. The
school policy is zero-tolerance for violence, meaning that children are
told not to return punches in a fight. Family values conflict directly with
school values. A principal can treat a situation in which a girl fights back
after being punched by suspending the child for three days, followed by
a meeting with her parents in which the principal explains school policy. This is treating the situation as a problem. Or the situation can be
treated as a dilemma in which particular family and school values con-

flict and have to be reconciled by determining where and under what conditions which values take precedence and different ways that a child and a family can learn to handle fights within the school.

No doubt many other questions will arise beyond these commonly asked ones. These questions can be answered by recalling the main points raised so far about solving problems and managing dilemmas. I summarize those points here:

1. Framing problems and dilemmas is subjective.
2. Solving problems and managing dilemmas means dealing with conflict.
3. How you frame a problem is crucial to finding solutions that work.
4. Poor problem or dilemma framing contains a ready-made solution or compromise within the definition. For example, the most common way to frame a problem in a classroom, school, or district is to blame a person or a group for causing the problem. Solution? Change the person's or group's behavior or get rid of the trouble-making party or parties.
5. Fault-free problem framing leaves much room for generating alternative solutions. Don't blame, reframe!
6. Some situations are so messy and intractable that they are not problems. They are dilemmas. Dilemmas have compromises, not solutions. Dilemmas are managed, not solved. Review the features of dilemmas.
7. If the problem or dilemma keeps returning, reframe the situation using other viewpoints.

❖ APPLYING PROBLEM AND DILEMMA FRAMING TO ACTUAL CASES

I have selected descriptions of problems that practitioners have written for my workshops over the years or that have been written by colleagues or myself. I have drawn examples from classrooms and schools in varied settings. Use the cases as opportunities to apply your knowledge and skills to distinguish between problems and dilemmas and to frame each better.

The Parent–Teacher Conference[18]

Ms. Glick was looking forward to the conference with Fazmina Muhammed's mother. Over the past year in her English class, she had seen how Fazmina had grown intellectually. Her skill in interpreting poems, short stories, and novels had improved substantially since she had arrived in Glick's class in September. In the beginning, Fazmina seldom spoke out in discussions, although her written work showed flashes of shrewd observations about people and carefully crafted prose. Now, with growing confidence, Fazmina was one of the top five contributors to class discussions, and other students listened carefully when she spoke. Fazmina was turning out to be the star of her class and one of the best students Glick had had since arriving at Glenville High School a decade earlier.

Glenville High was a school enrolling students from a low-income Latino barrio, with a sprinkling of African American and Middle Eastern students from adjacent neighborhoods. Glick taught the college-preparatory classes in English, and of her five daily classes, Fazmina was in one that met before lunch and had turned out to have an exciting mix of students. Many of them worked after school but loved the literature that Glick was showering over them. They had read *Wuthering Heights, Hamlet, The Scarlet Letter,* and dozens of short stories and poems.

Glick looked forward to the parent conference because she believed that Fazmina could get a partial—perhaps even a full—scholarship to a selective university, and she wanted to impress that upon her mother. She did have some concerns that arose from the few chats that she had had with Fazmina over bag lunches in the classroom. Every time Glick brought up the subject of college, Fazmina grew quiet and tried to change the subject. Glick had made sure that Fazmina had taken the SAT. (She had arranged with the counselor for the school to pay the test fee for Fazmina.) Fazmina had scored in the 1200s, with a 700 in the verbal section. When the topic of college arose, Glick didn't push Fazmina about her reluctance to discuss the matter, but she resolved to speak to the mother at the next parent conference.

To accommodate parent conferences for working mothers, fathers, and guardians, Glenville held potluck dinners two nights a week for a month (excusing teachers and students from school for a half-day each week) to permit at least half-hour conferences with parents who came.

Although Glick was tired by the second night of the third week of conferences, she eagerly looked forward to her conference with Fazmina's mother, Mrs. Muhammed.

Mrs. Muhammed, who appeared to be in her early 40s, arrived for the conference with a 3-year-old trailing after her. She made it clear to Glick that she wanted to hear both the good and bad about her oldest daughter's work in English. Glick launched into a rushed collection of stories about Fazmina's mature insights into literature, her analytic skills in reading poems and novels, and the marvelous growth that she had shown over the year. Fazmina, Glick said, was outstanding, a rising star in her five classes of 160 students.

Mrs. Muhammed glowed at Glick's words.

Then Glick began talking about the importance of Fazmina's continuing her education at the state university. She gave Mrs. Muhammed a printout of Fazmina's grade-point average (a B+), and showed the mother a university application and scholarship and financial-aid opportunities. The teacher told the mother that because she believed so strongly in Fazmina's capabilities for college, she would help her daughter complete all the forms for attending the university.

Mrs. Muhammed thanked Glick. She appreciated very much the fine words that the teacher offered in her daughter's behalf and the teacher's willingness to take the extra steps to help Fazmina. Then the mother quietly but forcefully explained to Glick that, as a single mother of four children (her husband had abandoned the family and had not been heard from for two years), she needed Fazmina to work and care for her younger sisters and brother. While members of her extended family occasionally helped out with food and clothes, the mother's income from her job as a cashier in the local supermarket was just barely adequate to pay the rent and put food on the table. In addition to the matter of insufficient money in the family, Mrs. Muhammed made it clear to the teacher that in her culture, as a young girl, she had been expected to help her parents out by caring for her younger brothers, and she did. So she expected the same from Fazmina. Going to college would be nice but a luxury, given the family's circumstances.

Glick was taken aback by the mother's insistence that Fazmina would find a job and also care for her younger siblings. The parent conference that she had so eagerly welcomed had turned out to be a disaster from her point of view. She was at a loss for words.

Questions

1. Is this a problem or a dilemma from Glick's viewpoint? Mrs. Muhammed's? Fazmina's? Yours? Explain your answers.
2. What is the relationship between a parent and a teacher in helping a student determine her future? Equal partners? Unequal partners? Explain your answer.
3. Reframe the problem or dilemma from another point of view.
4. What would you advise Glick to do in this situation? Elaborate your solution or compromise.

Placing Students at Christa McAuliffe Elementary School[19]

I was warned that there would be a great deal of parental pressure when I took this job as principal three years ago. During the first month on the job, I was bombarded by parental requests to have their children in specific teachers' classrooms in the fall. I inquired about a student-placement policy in the Water View Public School system, but there was none in writing.

Water View is a suburban and rural school district 30 miles southeast of a large city in a Midwestern state. It has five K–5 elementary schools, one grade 6–8 middle school, and one senior high school, for a total of about 5,000 students. Christa McAuliffe is the newest elementary school (1988) in this district. It was built on the growing west side of town, where a new shopping center, library, church, and expensive homes have been built. The district also draws from the rural part of the county. We have four classrooms per grade (class size is about 25 students). The school has almost 600 students. The staff is mature and well trained, and has been stable over the years.

Parental requests for specific teachers began in the district about 20 years ago. There were never more than a few such requests each year, and principals in the various schools could easily accommodate them. After McAuliffe opened, a very active parent group was formed, with an energetic leader who visited each classroom to find the "best" teacher for her children. Teachers resented this "evaluation" and continue to be wary of the parent leadership in the school. The parents created a form to use to make a request. Parental requests for particular teachers grew rapidly as the word spread among parents as to which teachers were perceived as "good," "mediocre," and "poor." Two years ago, there were 40 parental requests to fill 25 spaces in a popular 5th grade teacher's class. We had 125 requests from parents this past year.

Only the parents who seek out information about teachers or know other parents whose children have had good experiences in certain teachers' rooms make the requests. Of the 350 families served by the school, about 80 parents generate the requests. They assume, of course, that there is only one excellent teacher per grade.

I am now spending large chunks of my time considering requests from parents. Teachers complain about parents' lacking information about what occurs in their classrooms. Moreover, many of the teachers resent lay people judging professionals. Parents constantly call to see whether I have acted on their requests.

I brought this issue up to our principals' group last year and found that mine was the only school in the district where this was a problem. There were very few requests from parents for teachers in the other four schools. Nor did the principals wish to create a policy, because they believed such a policy would trigger a deluge of parental requests. I brought the matter to the superintendent, and he told me it was a "no-win situation," one that caused a principal in a nearby district to lose his job when he tried to eliminate parental requests. The matter was brought before our elementary principals' group again this past year; the result was a small modification of the "Teacher Request" form to include an educational reason for the request. This change has had little effect on the number or type of requests.

Questions

1. Is this a problem or dilemma for the principal? Explain your answer.
2. If you decided it was a dilemma, what values are in conflict?
3. Reframe the situation from another point of view.
4. What would you recommend the principal do?

The Trials of a First-Year Teacher[20]

Two impulses dominated Yvonne's first year as a teacher in the largely minority, poor school she had been assigned to. First, she wanted to be as good a teacher as her dad had been, and second, she wanted to help students, like herself, who endured the intentional and unintentional slights and scars that come with a dark skin. Yvonne came highly recommended by those who had worked with her in the state university's teacher-education program, and her strengths were evident to the department head who had recommended her to the principal for the position. Here was a young woman of color who had a dramatic presence and had successfully student-taught in a largely Latino high school. (Yvonne was also bilingual.)

Yvonne's first two months teaching five classes of U.S. history and world studies kept her whirling frantically through a blur of lessons. She had too little time to spend with individual students, and she worked late into the night preparing materials for class. Her strengths as a teacher soon became evident to her students, who spoke of her to their other teachers. She had a knack—unusual in a novice—for getting students to respond to her questions and probing their answers. She was comfortable waiting as long as three seconds for a student to answer, and she would coax an opinion or fact from even the shiest students. Also, she would often role-play a historical character. She used hats and scarves—even make-up—and her students listened to her as Frederick Douglass, Sojourner Truth, and Susan B. Anthony. She still had problems making smooth transitions from one activity to another; she sometimes forgot to give an assignment; and she seldom demanded from students what she had promised herself to ask for: brief written work that forced students to take positions on issues. She knew she still had a way to go to become a satisfactory teacher, but she at least saw the road ahead and felt that she could do it.

In November, during the height of the daily whirl, one of her 11th grade students, certainly not one of her best—Espy Mendoza—had come to her in tears just after school. Espy said that she had been suspended by the assistant principal because she had been rude to her Algebra teacher. Yvonne had had a few after-school conversations with Espy and had driven her home to a nearby public-housing project once when it was dark. Espy's mother had invited Yvonne to stay for dinner with the family, and she had stayed for a few hours.

Crying, Espy admitted that she had sworn at the teacher. She had been upset over an argument that she had just had with her boyfriend in the school's parking lot. Also, her father had refused to let her work at Wendy's the night before because of the late hours; there had been a terrible argument between her mother and father that had upset Espy. In class, the teacher had asked Espy twice to go to the chalkboard to do different homework problems. She told the teacher that she wasn't feeling well and asked whether she could pass. The teacher asked to see her homework, and Espy showed it to her. The teacher saw that the homework included correct answers to equations that, in the teacher's snap judgment, seemed beyond the work that Espy had usually done. Then the teacher, in a voice that could be heard across the room, accused her of not wanting to go the board because she had copied the answers and really didn't know how to do the problems. Espy had done the work herself. She felt humiliated. The anger rose in her throat; she lost control and swore at the teacher. The teacher ordered her out of the class, and she left. As upset as she was over the suspension, she was even more worried that her mother and father would be so angry with her that they would not let her go to a nearby community college after graduating.

When Yvonne spoke with Ms. Jackson, the veteran Algebra teacher, she expressed surprise at the blow-up. Espy had been a quiet, unobtrusive student. Yet Jackson was still very upset over the incident. Her account of what had happened in class agreed generally with Espy's. Jackson said that she did feel bad about making the accusation, but it was now water under the dam. Nevertheless, the teacher refused to ask the assistant principal to rescind the suspension.

Then Yvonne spoke with Ms. Alvarez, the assistant principal, about the suspension. She explained what Espy had said and offered to bring Espy in to apologize to the teacher and administrator. Alvarez was adamant, however, that a student who swore at a teacher in front of the class had to be punished with the one-day suspension. When Yvonne pulled the district's rules about due process in suspending students out of her backpack and asked whether the procedures had been followed, the assistant principal got very annoyed and said that they had. Yvonne noticed quickly that the administrator made notes and said coolly that she would take up the matter with the principal. She began working on forms on her desk, and Yvonne left.

That afternoon, after the last class ended, Espy ran into the room saying that she was no longer suspended. The assistant principal had called her in and said that if she apologized to the teacher, she could come to school the next day. Espy went to the algebra teacher, explained the situation at home and with her boyfriend, and said that she was very sorry for using the bad language and embarrassing her. Jackson accepted the apology.

In the next few months, Yvonne earned a reputation among those of her students who got into trouble with school administrators that she would stick up for them, provided that they told her the truth. This advocacy earned her no extra credit with school administrators, who tangled with the new teacher when she defended students who had broken school rules.

Nor did Yvonne's growing friendship with Juanita, Espy's mother, help the young woman reach her goal of becoming a first-rate teacher. Juanita asked Yvonne for help in organizing a new tenants' council for the housing project because the old one just did what the manager wanted, and maintenance and repairs had deteriorated badly. Yvonne got in touch with a college friend who had become a community organizer in a nearby city.

Between January and March, for one night a week, Yvonne, Juanita, and a small group of women, mostly single Latino and African American mothers, began planning to oust the existing tenants' council in the annual May election. These meetings lasted three or more hours an evening and took a lot out of Yvonne. The mothers wanted her to take leadership of the group because of her education, but she had been warned repeatedly by her friend to push for the leadership to come from the women; she would advise and consult with the leaders. This was hard for Yvonne to do, and she had to think about tactics repeatedly, even while she was teaching.

By late April, Yvonne's teaching, helping students who had been in trouble with school authorities, and work with the tenants' group had high and low points. One high point was that Yvonne decided to drop a unit on the 1920s and replace it with a unit that she was developing about urban problems since World War II, with a focus on housing. The low point was the obvious personal toll that all of her work had taken. She was thoroughly fatigued. She was too tired to call her closest friend or even her parents. Not enough sleep because of frequent phone calls at night from students and Juanita left Yvonne dragging each day. Then, late on a Thursday afternoon, Yvonne's classroom phone rang, and the principal's secretary called to say that Dr. Washington wanted to see her immediately after class.

Yvonne went to the office. She was apprehensive because it was the first face-to-face meeting that she had had with the principal and didn't know why she had been called. Washington smiled when he saw Yvonne. He began by saying how pleased he was with reports from the department head and a few parents of students that she was doing so well as a teacher. She knew her subject matter and managed the class without sending students to the assistant principal. He said that she had a fine career ahead of her. Then he said "but," and Yvonne knew before he said another word that her other activities were really the basis for the meeting.

Washington launched into an accounting of the cases of seven students who had been suspended or threatened by suspension in which Yvonne had intervened. Alvarez had complained to him every time the young teacher's intervention made her job more difficult, saying that these students were low performers academically and troublemakers who cared little about graduating. Moreover, Washington had gotten a call from the manager of the public-housing project, who said that one of his teachers was organizing a group of tenants to get rid of the existing council. The manager felt that the teacher had no business working with his tenants and wanted her to stop meeting with the group.

Yvonne had known that all of this might happen. She had considered the risks early on and felt strongly that she could (and should) be the kind of activist teacher who would be a role model for her students. She wanted to do all of these things, even though she knew how much of a mental and physical toll the work was taking on her.

Washington looked Yvonne straight in the eyes and said: "Yvonne, I want you to stay on this staff. You have a bright future as a teacher. But this child advocacy and tenant organizing has to stop. Now, I can't tell you what to do in your own time after school, but if I see that it affects your work as a teacher negatively, then I will intervene. As for being an advocate of certain students against administrators who are just trying to do the job that I assign them, let me tell you that I won't tolerate it. Yes, we make occasional mistakes, but in a school of 1,500 teenagers, we must have order, because the homes and streets that many of our students return to are disorganized and even dangerous. Here at school, at least, there is some stability. Your advocacy threatens that. I wanted you to know what my position is on these matters. Now, what do you have to say?"

Questions

1. Is the situation that Yvonne faces largely a problem or a dilemma? If you decide it is a dilemma, be specific as to listing the values that she prizes most highly.
2. Suppose that Yvonne has asked Washington for a little time to think about responding, and he has scheduled a meeting first thing in the morning. Yvonne calls you, her best friend, explains the situation, and asks for your advice. What would you advise her to say to the principal? Be detailed in your answer.
3. Reframe the problem or dilemma from another point of view.
4. Have you ever faced such a situation? Explain the circumstances.

PART II ❖

Change

Few practitioners make the explicit connection that problem
solving and managing dilemmas are about change. What most
teachers and administrators forget is that every planned
change, every so-called reform, is a solution to some problem
or a compromise for some dilemma. Show me a reform and
I will show you a problem that it is supposed to solve or a
dilemma it is supposed to finesse. Solving a tame problem or
constructing a compromise to a dilemma means that something has to change somewhere. Note how many of the examples I have used involved change. Thus, solving problems and
managing dilemmas lead inexorably to change. This section
deals with change within classrooms, schools, and districts.

❖ THINKING AND DOING CHANGE

Most practitioners have had many experiences with
planned changes in classrooms and schools that they have ini-
tiated or that have been hurled at them. Teachers and principals can tell story after story about both exhilarating involvement in a reform and botched efforts. Contrary to popular
claims that schools are traditional institutions that hardly
ever change, practitioners can testify to their involvement in
national, state, and local reforms and in designing changes in
their classrooms and schools. Both stability and change char-
acterize American schools.[21]

Certainly, many changes disappear after a while, offering
evidence of stability, but some innovations are incorporated
into routine classroom and school operations. At one time,

for example, there were one-room schoolhouses; today, the age-graded school dominates. At one time, only a one-size-fits-all curriculum was available for high-school students; today, many choices are available to students. At one time, teachers taught the entire class as one group, day in and day out; today, teachers use small groups, independent work, and large-group instruction. Historically and contemporaneously, school staffs mix constancy and change in carrying out their assigned duties. Nevertheless, popular opinion has it that schools seldom change, and when they do, practitioners are criticized for not changing more frequently and moving in particular directions. Why is that?[22]

Part of any answer to this question has to include how highly prized the idea of change is in society. To put it bluntly: Americans believe that change is good. To see that change is so highly valued, we need look no farther than commonplace patterns that pervade our daily lives. Dress hems move up and down; men's ties get fatter and thinner. Car models change every year. Elections move public officials in and out of office every few years. And Americans love to move from where they were reared to other places. Change, then, is common; it is no big deal.

Another part of an answer is that many practitioners confuse change with improvement. They are different concepts. When a sweet, smart, easy-to-handle 10-year-old daughter turns into a cursing, disobedient, angry 13-year-old, there certainly has been change—but to the parents, there has hardly been an improvement. When a married couple divorces, one spouse can see it as joyful emancipation while the other sees it as a tragedy. That is, the divorce qualifies as a change, but each spouse views it dramatically differently. Change, therefore, is not necessarily improvement. Improvement is in the head of the beholder.

Translated to public schools, planned changes that were meant to strengthen the curriculum or school organization are implemented, but no improvements emerge. Problems persist. Promoters' high expectations are dashed. The planned changes are seen as failures. Traditional ways trump improvements.

So practitioners are often criticized for being opposed to change when their fellow Americans see change as a highly valued good, one that automatically leads to improvement. Keeping this explanation in mind (it is not the only one that can be offered but will do for now), I will concentrate on different kinds of planned changes that have occupied practitioners for decades.[23]

❖ TYPES OF PLANNED CHANGE

The distinctions I draw among types of planned change have been most helpful to me as a teacher, superintendent, and professor. By seeing planned changes or reforms as solutions to problems, I have been able to ask teachers and principals: To what problem is this change a solution? These distinctions have helped me think through the connections among solving problem, managing dilemmas, and making changes in classrooms and schools.

To understand the deeper meanings of past and current efforts to change schools and classroom teaching and to connect broad policies of school improvement with classroom teachers' behavior, I distinguish between two kinds of planned change: incremental and fundamental.

Incremental Changes

These changes aim to improve the inefficiency and ineffectiveness of existing structures and cultures of schooling, including classroom teaching. By structures, I mean the goals, funding, facilities, and age-graded schools that are basic building blocks of the system of tax-supported schooling in the United States. By cultures, I mean the norms, expectations, and beliefs in the classroom, school, and district that color the daily activities of children and adults in schools (see Figure 3).

Designers of incremental change view the basic structures and cultures of schooling as largely sound but in need of improvement. There are problems, inefficiencies, and ineffective practices that undermine the productivity of the system. These problems can be solved. The old car, to use a familiar metaphor, is sputtering and rusting but solid. It needs a paint job, tires, brakes, a new battery, and a tune-up—incremental changes. Once improved, the system will work as intended.

Examples of incremental changes in schools would include adding new courses to a curriculum; introducing a new standardized test; adopting merit pay for teachers and principals; decreasing class size from 30 to 25; adding two more counselors to a secondary school; and changing the parent-conference schedule to accommodate single and working parents. Each of these changes is, of course, a solution to a problem identified by individuals and different groups.

In the classroom, incremental changes would include a teacher's introducing a new unit in her math course that she has never taught before or designing a behavior-modification plan with escalating rewards and penalties for good and bad classroom behavior. A teacher's deciding to accept the offer of a computer for his classroom to keep attendance and grades more efficiently and communicate with colleagues is another example.

Fundamental Changes

These changes aim to transform—alter permanently—those very same structures and cultures described earlier and in Figure 3. The idea behind fundamental change is that the basic structures and cultures are irretrievably flawed at their core and need a complete overhaul or replacement, not improvement. That old car is a jalopy far beyond repair. We need to get a new car or consider other forms of transportation.

New courses, more staff, summer school, and higher salaries for teachers are examples of incremental changes in the structures and cultures of schooling. The late-19th-century innovation of the kindergarten, on the other hand, is an instance of fundamental change. Other examples would be the broadening of the school's social role in the early 20th century to intervene in the lives of children and their families (e.g., offering school-based social and medical services) and for advocates of public schooling to see the institution as an agent of social reform in the larger society (e.g., ending alcohol and drug abuse, desegregation). Advocates of vouchers and charter schools want to end the monopoly that states have on public schooling by altering the fundamental structure of funding, thus permitting more choice. Other reformers seeking nongraded schools, for example, wish to replace the century-and-a-half-old age-graded school with a new organization that eliminates promotion and retention, the segmented curriculum, and self-contained classrooms. Again, changes designed as fundamental are proposed solutions to deep-seated problems or intractable dilemmas.

As applied to the classroom, advocates of fundamental change would aim to transform the teacher's role from central source of power and knowledge to that of a coach who guides students to their own decisions—who helps children find meaning in their experiences and urges them to learn from one another and from other sources. These reform-

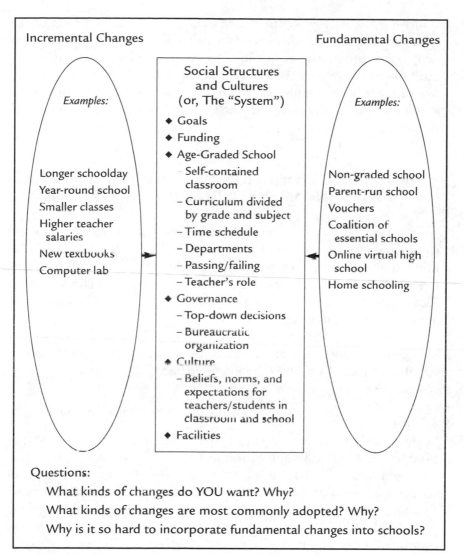

Incremental Changes

Fundamental Changes

Examples:

Longer schoolday
Year-round school
Smaller classes
Higher teacher
  salaries
New textbooks
Computer lab

Social Structures
and Cultures
(or, The "System")

◆ Goals
◆ Funding
◆ Age-Graded School
  – Self-contained
    classroom
  – Curriculum divided
    by grade and subject
  – Time schedule
  – Departments
  – Passing/failing
  – Teacher's role
◆ Governance
  – Top-down decisions
  – Bureaucratic
    organization
◆ Culture
  – Beliefs, norms, and
    expectations for
    teachers/students in
    classroom and school
◆ Facilities

Examples:

Non-graded school
Parent-run school
Vouchers
Coalition of
  essential schools
Online virtual high
  school
Home schooling

Questions:

What kinds of changes do YOU want? Why?

What kinds of changes are most commonly adopted? Why?

Why is it so hard to incorporate fundamental changes into schools?

FIGURE 3. What Kinds of Change Do You Want?

ers seek to end the traditional version of teaching in which the teacher does most of the talking, students mostly listen, a textbook is relied on as the main source of knowledge, and tests are given to determine how much has been remembered. The reformers seek to replace traditional teaching with classrooms in which teachers organize activities that help students learn from subject matter, one another, and the community. Student learning becomes active and includes group work, play, independent work, and artistic expression. Assessment is based less on taking multiple-choice tests than on completing real-world tasks. Such changes would mean fundamental alterations in the ways that teachers think about the nature of knowledge, teaching, and learning, and about their actions in the classroom.

❖ IS THE DISTINCTION BETWEEN INCREMENTAL AND FUNDAMENTAL CHANGE IMPORTANT?

Figure 3 locates the basic structures and cultures of schooling and summarizes the incremental and fundamental changes intended to alter them. I offer additional examples in the figure. If you want to pause and reflect on what you have read and connect your experiences to these ideas, note the questions at the bottom of the figure and jot down your answers before reading further.

In examining the history of these two different kinds of planned changes in schools and classrooms, certain lessons have become apparent about incremental and fundamental changes.[24]

Most fundamental changes initially come from outside the schools.

The Civil Rights Movement of the 1950s and 1960s, for example, prodded public officials and educators to respond to the inequities that civil-rights leaders and demonstrators outlined in their protests over poor facilities, unequal treatment in schools, and low academic achievement. In addition, heavy corporate involvement in public schools since the early 1980s, which has been aimed at wedding schools more closely to improving the economy, has led to the introduction of business practices, new technology, and other private-sector innovations.

Many changes intended to be fundamental become incrementalized.

Often the words surrounding a planned change clearly intend to make profound shifts in the current school. Recall the promotion of school-based management, middle schools, the new math, and personal computers in the 1980s and 1990s. These innovations promoted by corporate leaders and public officials outside the schools sought to make fundamental changes. Yet once these innovations left the designers' hands and entered the schools and classrooms, they were either partially or moderately implemented—or, in some instances, they were never put into practice. In many junior high schools seeking to become middle schools in ideology and practice, for example, administrators and faculty picked and chose among the features of a middle school—say, a block schedule—but ignored each student's having an adviser, interdisciplinary teaching, and traditional forms of teaching.

Because so much work is involved in mobilizing support and resources for fundamental changes, there is far more success in talking about major reforms than in designing and adopting the planned changes. And there is even more of a gap between the policy actions taken by public officials and what principals and teachers actually put into practice. Because of these gaps among talk, action, and implementation, intended fundamental changes get incrementalized and become another enhancement to the existing organizational structures and processes.

Far more incremental than fundamental changes get institutionalized in schools.

It is simply easier, organizationally and psychologically, to add to existing structures, processes, and cultures than to erase or redirect those systemic components. Creating a new course to add to an existing curriculum stirs less conflict than eliminating a curriculum or building a new one from the ground up. Increasing requirements for high-school graduation takes work in building support for such a measure but differs greatly from eliminating the Carnegie unit, which is the basis of counting credits toward graduation. Shipping computers to schools and buying software is far easier than altering dominant teaching practices

❖ APPLYING CONCEPTS OF CHANGE TO ACTUAL CASES

In working with almost 1,000 teachers, principals, superintendents, and school-board members in California, Minnesota, Washington, New York, and Virginia over the years, I have asked them to tell me where, in their heart of hearts, they stand on the kind of change they seek in schools. I have asked each person to pick a spot along the continuum of incremental to fundamental change. Almost two-thirds chose the fundamental side of the continuum.

But practitioners argued with me that choosing along the one continuum was too crude. These teachers and administrators knew that districts and schools were organizations that solved problems fitfully and slowly. They wanted a choice that better fit their experiences than a forced choice along one continuum. They wanted to combine incremental and fundamental with different ways to achieve these changes. In short, they recognized that strategies of change also mattered.

To accommodate their wishes, I combined types of change and different implementation strategies into one matrix. Thus, I offered them a choice of strategies to implement the changes they desired—that is, make the changes in small steps or make the changes in one fell swoop or in grand moves (see Figure 4).

To illustrate some of the practitioners' choices, consider a kindergarten teacher—call her Lisa—who put herself in the A quadrant. (Where in the quadrant she placed her name—in the middle or close to B, C, or D—indicates where her blend of inclinations rested.) Lisa was an incrementalist who defined a problem in her teaching as not giving her 5-year-olds experience with new technology. She wanted to introduce computers in her kindergarten class by having one installed in the current year and a second the following year. She would set up a computer center, just like her centers for blocks, art, literacy, and science.

Steve, a high-school principal, placed himself in the C quadrant. In January, he had decided that, in September, his high school would introduce a block schedule of three daily 90-minute periods, because he was convinced that this would make the teaching and learning more efficient than the current seven periods of 48 minutes each. He concentrated only on the change in the schedule; he wanted to maintain existing departments and avoided questioning teachers about what they would do in the 90-minute block. Within six weeks he had mobilized a faculty group in support of the change, solved the logistical problems teachers identified, found the appropriate software to make the changes over the summer, and got the school-site committee to endorse it. He wrote a proposal that was funded for half of the staff to spend two weeks during the summer planning for activities in each academic subject that could be adapted to longer periods.

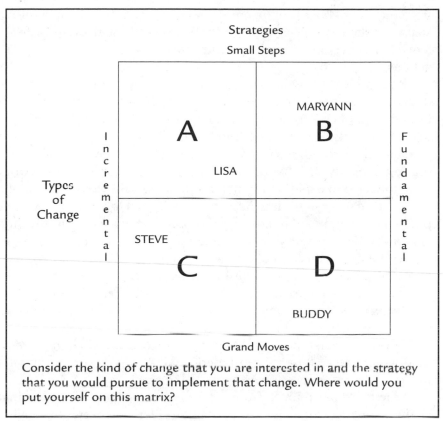

FIGURE 4. Change: Types and Strategies

A and C are incrementalist quadrants; B and D belong to those who, in their hearts, seek fundamental changes in their classroom, school, or district, but at different paces. Maryann, a veteran elementary-school principal in a largely Latino barrio, confidently wrote her name in the B quadrant. The problem in her school, as she framed it, was that the enrollment was rapidly becoming majority Latino and segregated from the rest of society. She sought to make her school into a dual immersion school (Spanish and English), where the language skills and culture of her families and students could be used to the fullest so that the non-Latino children could be educated and the Latino children could learn from others who were unlike themselves. She wanted this innovation passionately but knew that it would take at least three years to get approval from the school board and to enroll the students. She laid out all of the steps that she would have to follow each year and listed all of the problems that she could anticipate. She knew what she wanted and how to get there.

Buddy dashed his name into quadrant D with a flourish. A science teacher, Buddy had become convinced that his customary way to teach biology and chemistry was inadequate for the increasingly culturally diverse students he saw before him each year. He was a great believer in students' discovering scientific concepts for themselves and in working in teams on projects, yet he was still tied to lectures, homework from the textbook, and occasional lab periods. Buddy wanted to make a dramatic change in his teaching. In April, he had located 10 new computers and a handful of biology software programs that were nicely integrated with key units that he would teach, and he found a young biology teacher in another school who agreed to help him learn the software. Over the summer, working with his colleague, Buddy reorganized the standard biology course he had offered. In September, with the help of a computer-savvy senior, Buddy put half of the class on the computers—students were able to turn to the senior for help—while Buddy concentrated on the half-dozen students who needed extra help from him. In the past, such students had fallen behind quickly and eventually failed.

Wherever a practitioner chose to put his or her name, it was clear that change, solving problems, and managing dilemmas were thoroughly entangled. Invariably, a planned change was a solution to a problem or a compromise to a dilemma that the teacher, principal, or someone else had framed. Also, the change itself, as it was adopted and implemented, invariably generated other problems and dilemmas. The deeply entangled process of solving problems, reconciling dilemmas, and making changes is perpetual.

I have selected descriptions of planned changes that practitioners have written for my workshops or that I have created based on the experiences that practitioners described. I have drawn examples from classrooms and schools in varied settings. Use the cases as opportunities to apply your knowledge and skills to distinguish between incremental and fundamental changes and the strategies that you would use to make the change happen. Note which problems and dilemmas would arise in the adoption and implementation of the planned change.

Making Hummer a Good School[25]

Hummer Middle School is located in a middle-class suburb of a Northwestern city and has 25 teachers. Despite the middle-class surroundings, more than 30 percent of the school's 500 students in grades 6 through 8 come from families that have recently immigrated from countries in Asia and speak English as a second language. These families depend on public assistance and help from the school to pay many extra fees levied by the school. Another 15 percent of the students, many of them from other parts of the suburb, have been assigned to Hummer because they had trouble adjusting to their original schools.

Academically, the school has been sliding downward for the past five years. Once the top school academically and in the fine arts among the four middle schools in the district, Hummer has fallen to the bottom in reading and math scores on a national standardized test. The school no longer holds an annual arts festival or four plays a year—features that once brought people to Hummer from all over the metropolitan area. According to veteran teachers, discipline has broken down in many classrooms, and many teachers now close their doors and cover the windows on their doors so that students roaming the halls won't look in or interrupt the class. Teacher turnover has increased, and the central administration is making matters worse by assigning inexperienced teachers to the school.

The superintendent brought the current principal to the school four years earlier because of difficulties that this principal had encountered at one of the district's high schools. According to veteran teachers, the school's climate has turned authoritarian, with the principal delegating disciplinary authority to two inexperienced assistant principals who also were assigned to the school within the past year. Even well-behaved students view the administration as heavy-handed and resent the hallway monitors, the constant need for passes to go to the bathroom, and the practice of keeping outside doors locked to prevent non-students from entering the school.

In the latest accreditation report, which has placed Hummer on academic probation for five years, the Visiting Committee explicitly mentions that students in classes they visited were openly bored. Many students are failing courses. The committee notes in its report that "rigid adherence to academic standards and traditional disciplines leaves many students feeling left out and failing." The committee report includes a quote from the science department's chair: "It's OK to fail 25 percent of the students; they won't amount to much anyway."

The increasing teacher turnover worries the committee, which points out that transfers to other schools have decimated the veteran staff. Moreover, for those teachers who have remained, the principal's lack of support for professional development, the fine arts program, and academic progress has left what was once a stable staff in deep gloom about the future.

The committee also expresses deep concern over the lack of parent participation and feels that the school's administration is going out of its way to discourage parents from getting involved in school affairs. The committee notes that the Parent–Teacher Organization is defunct, and that the principal has yet to fill five parent vacancies on the school-site committee, which is mandated by the district.

When the superintendent presents the Visiting Committee's final accreditation report on Hummer Middle School to the Board of Education, there is an immediate uproar in the community. No suburban school has ever been placed on academic probation before. Both the superintendent and the principal are severely criticized in the local newspaper and in an open session of the Board of Education at which parents speak.

Within six months, the Board of Education has fired the superintendent and appointed as his successor a veteran principal of a high school who had been principal of Hummer in better days. The top goal of the new superintendent (and the Board of Education) is to get Hummer off academic probation and make it a good school again.

Imagine that the new superintendent has hired you as a consultant to identify the most serious issues at Hummer and the changes that have to be made for the school to become one in which students, parents, and teachers can take pride. The contract that the Board of Education has offered asks that you perform the following tasks:

1. Identify the most serious problems that need immediate attention.
2. Identify those problems that are long term and will have to be dealt with eventually.
3. Design a five-year plan that will solve the problems as outlined in the example; remove Hummer from academic probation; and produce satisfaction with the school among students, teachers, and parents.

As a consultant, you are not restricted to identifying problems. If you see dilemmas, educate the Board of Education about what they are. Also, you will need to distinguish between incremental and fundamental changes that may be have to be made at Hummer and the strategies that you would use.

Janice Sunshine's 5th Grade Class

So much had happened at the David Mazer Elementary School in the past five years. Sondra Hilo, the new principal of the urban school, is committed to using technology in classrooms. She has written grants to secure new equipment, lobbied local merchants to underwrite new wiring of the school, and persuaded the Parent–Teachers Organization to purchase laptop computers.

Within a year, she has produced an extraordinary outpouring of desktop and laptop computers for the 400-student school. By the beginning of her second year, each of the 20 classrooms has five up-to-date computers, a printer, and a digital camera. There is one lab with 25 computers, a printer, and a server, and media center has a bank of 20 machines with similar attachments. The ratio of students to computers is lower than 3:1, the best among the city's schools. What Hilo wants is for every teacher to be an active user of computers in his or her classroom—even Janice Sunshine.

Janice Sunshine is a veteran, no-nonsense 5th grade teacher who is highly regarded by parents and who leads a small group of teachers who have been at the school for almost 20 years. Sunshine prides herself on getting students ready for 6th grade in math, science, and social studies. She has taken university courses in these subjects for the past few years and has even taught district courses for other teachers in strengthening the critical thinking skills of elementary-school students.

In her classroom, Sunshine intersperses whole-group discussions with brief lectures, occasional small-group work, and independent projects. She maintains iron-clad discipline that students, year after year, feel is strict but fair. At any given moment, a student or visitor can look at the chalkboard and see the daily schedule showing which activity is next. Charts of students' progress in math, science, and social-studies work are arrayed on the walls so that all students can see what they have accomplished and what remains to be done.

Then, one mid-September day, two men deliver five computers, a printer, and a digital camera to the classroom.

Sunshine has listened to the new principal expound on the importance of computers in school to prepare children for an information-based society and do research on the Internet. Two of her teaching colleagues have purchased computers and rave about e-mail, shopping on the Internet, and using the machines to handle personal finances. Sunshine is curious, but her life is so busy now, between school and her family (she had two teenage daughters), that the thought of learning how to use computers, finding software, and figuring out how to work the machines into her daily teaching simply overwhelms her. So she puts the boxes in the back of the room and leaves them there for the rest of September and all of October.

In late September and early October, Hilo arranges for a three-day in-school workshop for teachers who want to use the computers. The workshop is led by a well-respected teacher whom Sunshine knows. Sunshine attends the workshop and is surprised by all of the activities that students can do for themselves, the range of software that the school already has, and the quality of work that students have produced in her colleague's class. The principal also hires an instructional technician for the 10 teachers who have already started using their computers in classrooms, and she offers to pay for substitutes for any Mazer teacher who wants to visit other teachers in the district who use computers regularly.

Sunshine and a colleague visit a few schools with similar enrollments to Mazer's. They see comparable classes working on computers and producing work that exceeds what their students are doing. They also see that these teachers have organized their classes and daily schedules very differently from those of Sunshine and other teachers. Also, there is more noise in the room. Students walk around a great deal, talk about what is on their screens, and help one another. The students do, however, seem to be highly engaged with the machines, on task, and with one another in ways that Sunshine has seen in her room only occasionally.

Even though she is still concerned about the changes in organization and scheduling that will have to occur in her classroom, Sunshine nevertheless finds her curiosity piqued. She borrows one of the laptops available to teachers from the instructional technician. For three straight weeks, she spends an hour a night playing with the different software programs loaded on the machine; searching the Internet; using e-mail; playing the children's games; and working with programs geared for elementary-school math and science. Her daughters help her find science, math, and social-studies Web sites that have lessons and material that she can download. She is stunned by the high quality of the programs and the wealth of information she has at the click of a mouse. She sees that some of the software can be very helpful to her students, and she can see her students doing research on the Web.

But she also sees the complexity of using the software in her class when she is also expected by the principal, the school board, and her own standards to cover so much other content, prepare students for district tests, and make sure that her students are ready for the 6th grade in June. She sees the virtues of using computers in her classroom, but she also still sees their use as an add-on. The work will be something extra for her to do.

Sunshine also worries about organizing the class of 20 when she has only five computers. Even with two students at a computer, that will mean half of the class will be on computers and half will be engaged in other activities. Although she has used small-group work before, this is different, because the software is interactive and students have to respond to the questions and commands of the program. Students will be asking her questions all the time, and she is not sure she will be able to answer them all. Yes, two of her students have computers at home and are wizards with the machines. She has asked them for help on numerous occasions, and they have taught her a lot already.

Still, something is disturbing to her that she cannot put her finger on. Will she still be in charge when the 5th graders work on computers, when they help one another, or when she turns to a few students to answer questions about the software, using the digital camera, and fixing the printer when it breaks down? She had prided herself on her control of 5th graders: A raised eyebrow, a pointed finger, or a whispered command from her dissolves potential misbehavior.

On several occasions, Hilo stops in and watches Sunshine teach. In early November, the principal sees that Sunshine had cordoned off space in the classroom for the computers and printers. She also sees that Sunshine has slightly altered her traditional schedule: She allows a half-hour in the afternoon for computer time. Half the class works on a chapter in the science text, and half works with a science software program that is connected to the chapter in the text. Sunshine makes sure that in each group working on the computers, one of the computer wizards is appointed student-assistant to help those who have questions.

Hilo wonders just how far Sunshine will go in using computers in her classroom. Are these changes the beginning or the end of the process? Because many of the other teachers look to Sunshine as a leader, and the principal dearly wants to recruit this fine teacher as a serious computer user, the next few months have much riding on them.

Questions

1. What problem, if any, does Sunshine face? Is there a dilemma? Elaborate.
2. What kinds of changes does Sunshine make by Hilo's visit in early November? Explain.
3. Were Sunshine to keep making small changes in her daily schedule, classroom organization, and relationships with students, what kinds of accumulated changes would these be? Explain your answer.
4. Where would you place Sunshine on Figure 4? Why?

The Case of the Disappointed High-School Department Head: My Answers to Questions

1. Is this a routine problem or a dilemma? Explain your answer.

To me, this is no routine problem. It is a dilemma. The conflicting values are strewn throughout the description of the situation at Larchmont High School. Here is a short list of those value conflicts:

a. Reed values highly student-centered teaching practices; the veteran social-studies teachers largely favor subject-centered teaching practices.

b. Individual teachers value their pedagogical autonomy within the classroom and feel minimal obligation to the chair or even the principal when it comes to changing their teaching practices. Reed and the principal also value this autonomy but see it as conflicting with the professional obligations that teachers have to district authorities (who pay their salaries) for improving not only the students' performance but also the department's performance.

c. The teachers prize highly individual excellence in students' academic performance; Reed and the principal, concerned about declining student performance, prize equity and raising the bottom half of students who are doing poorly in academics.

Given these value clashes (and there are others), I would have to figure out which were primary and secondary clashes and frame the dilemma so that it would focus on the primary value conflict.

2. *According to Reed, what is the problem that has to be solved? Explain your reasoning. Evidence?*

Even though I see the situation more as a dilemma than a problem, I also would guess that Reed (and the principal, see question 4) view the situation as a problem. My hunch is that both would frame the problem in a similar manner: How do we get these veteran social-studies teachers who largely teach in traditional ways to change their practices to more active learning by students?

Both Reed, as department chair, and the principal implicitly link the large number of failing students to the use of traditional teaching practices with a culturally diverse population. This linkage may or may not exist or even be consistent with findings from research studies, but it is a connection that informs how both frame the problem. In effect, they blame the teachers for using inappropriate teaching practices.

By defining the problem in this manner, the solution becomes self-evident: change the teaching practices of the veteran social-studies teachers. The strategies Reed used were reasonable and even imaginative, but after one year they were failing.

3. *What would you guess Tom, Steve, John, or any of the other veteran teachers in the department would say is the primary problem that has to be solved? Explain your reasoning. Evidence?*

I would guess that Tom, Steve, John, and the department's other veteran teachers would say that the primary problem that has to be solved is getting rid of Reed and putting Tom Yarney, the AP American government teacher, into the position of department chair. To the teachers, Reed has invaded their pedagogical privacy and intervened in professional matters that are not her business.

If we pushed these teachers to state the core problem, they might say that demographic changes would continue to contribute heavily to the decline in students' academic performance, even if Reed disappeared. They probably would not see the problem in terms of how teachers teach their classes.

4. *What would you guess the principal would say is the primary problem that has to be solved? Explain your reasoning. Evidence?*

See my answer to the first question.

5. *If you decided that this was a routine problem, how would you frame it? If you decided that it was a dilemma, how would you frame it?*

As I indicated in my answer to the first question, I see this situation as a dilemma, not a routine problem. I would frame the dilemma in this way: In what ways, if at all, would student-centered teaching practices decrease the high number of students failing to attend class (69 percent) and those receiving Ds or Fs in social-studies courses (42 percent)? The virtue of framing the dilemma in this manner is that it deals directly with the assumptions that the principal and department chair have about the relationship between teaching practices and student outcomes. Moreover, stating the dilemma in this manner puts the focus on student behavior and performance and allows results to be assessed. Also, stating the dilemma this way does not attack the teachers; in fact, it demands that Reed and the principal show evidence of the connection between teachers' practices and students' outcomes. Reed could do this by researching cooperative learning in secondary schools, by having the teachers visit high-achieving teachers in other schools with similar enrollments, or by bringing in colleagues from other departments at Larchmont whose students come to school regularly and whose grades are satisfactory.

Would framing the dilemma in this manner magically erase the issues that the veteran social-studies teachers have raised? Hardly. The value conflict between subject-centered and student-centered teaching practices will remain. In defining the dilemma in this manner, however, Reed acknowledges that there is a value conflict and takes on the burden of making the case for diversifying her social-studies teachers' repertoires without blaming them for causing the unsatisfactory student outcomes.

Reframing the Dilemma of the Disappointed High-School Department Head

In Appendix A, I avoided using a psychological perspective to define the dilemma that Phyllis Reed and the principal faced at Larchmont. Had I used that point of view, I would have concentrated on the personal traits and behaviors of the teachers that were causing unsatisfactory student outcomes. Instead, I framed the dilemma by using the classroom as an organization and connected how teachers taught within that organizational setting to certain student outcomes. Both the principal and Phyllis Reed assumed such a connection but did not make it explicit. They assumed that the teachers' organization of their classrooms, the dominant teaching practices, the climate in the classrooms, and the teachers' relationships with the students were linked strongly to the students' behavior and academic performance.

To reframe the dilemma, I will use both organizational and political perspectives. Here is how I would state the reframed dilemma:

> *What are the organizational incentives and sanctions that the principal can use to move all departments toward designing changes aimed at improving student attendance and academic performance?*

Reframing the dilemma in this manner allows the situation to be viewed as a schoolwide dilemma, not a dilemma restricted to the social-studies department. It is an organizational dilemma, not one faced alone by Phyllis Reed. Moreover, it recognizes that the obligation to work toward improvement of student outcomes—a highly charged and important value—may well interfere with and diminish the value of individual teachers' autonomy. Furthermore, reframing brings the value of equity back into the conversation within the school, replacing the concentration on individual excellence that gets translated as, "Those who succeed are fine; the rest can't make it."

By invoking organizational incentives and sanctions, the principal recognizes that there are incentives to which many teachers in the school will respond: providing extra funds for departments and time for teachers to visit other schools; reducing teaching loads so that teachers can analyze student attendance and letter-grade distributions subject by subject; and redefining the role of department chair as a more influential figure within the department and the school. The principal also recognizes that using his power to evaluate teacher's performance, to negotiate changes in teachers' schedules, and to hire new teachers and transfer other teachers into different assignments gives him political leverage to move the staff toward the changes that he seeks.

Notes

1. Within professions and academic disciplines, the framing and solving of problems differ. For the most part, psychologists have dominated the literature on problem solving and initially laid out a rational, step-by-step process of identifying a situation as a problem; generating alternatives; choosing the best option; implementing the choice; and determining whether the problem has been solved. Although many disciplines still adhere to this rational problem-solving process, sophisticated, in-depth studies of practitioners have been conducted that reveal more twists and turns then the steps would suggest. How teachers, architects, psychotherapists, physicians, engineers, and policymakers frame and solve problems varies by occupation but contains generic similarities. For an example of the psychologist literature on problem solving, see R. Mayer, *Thinking, problem solving, cognition*, 2nd ed. (New York: W. H. Freeman, 1992); for an example of how different professionals, from architects to engineers, physicians, and town planners, identify problems and work them through within their occupation, see D. Schön, *The reflective practitioner: How professionals think in action* (New York: Basic Books, 1983); for one type of psychotherapist, see J. Haley, *Problem-solving therapy* (New York: Harper and Row, 1976); for principals and superintendents, see K. Leithwood & R. Steinbach, *Expert problem solving: Evidence from school and district leaders* (Albany: State University of New York Press, 1995); for physicians, see L. Shulman & A. Elstein, *Medical problem solving* (Cambridge, MA: Harvard University Press, 1978); for policymakers, see J. Kingdon, *Agendas, alternatives, and public pPolicies*, 2nd ed. (New York: HarperCollins College Publishers, 1995).

2. These steps often appear in books devoted to problem solving. See, for example, J. Dewey, *How we think* (Boston: D. C. Heath, 1933); J. Hayes, *The complete problem solver* (Philadelphia: Franklin Institute, 1981); A. Gaynor, *Analyzing problems in schools and school systems* (Mahwah, NJ: Lawrence Erlbaum Associates, 1998).

3. The Einstein quote is cited (p. 37) in J. W. Getzels, The problem of the problem, in R. Hogarth (Ed.), *New directions for methodology of social and behavioral science: Question framing and response consistency*, no. 11 (San Francisco: Jossey-Bass, March 1982), 37–49.

4. R. Mason & I. Mitroff distinguish between tame and wicked problems. See *Challenging strategic planning assumptions: Theory, cases, and techniques* (New York: John Wiley & Sons, 1981), 10–13.

5. For constructing this view of dilemmas, I have used the following sources: A. Berlak & H. Berlak, *Dilemmas of schooling* (London: Methuen, 1981); M. Billig, S. Condor, D. Edwards, M. Gane, D. Middleton, & A. Radley, *Ideological dilemmas: A social psychology of everyday thinking* (Newbury Park, CA: SAGE Publications, 1988); P. Elbow, Embracing contraries in the teaching process, *College English, 45*(4), 327–339; S. Sarason, *The culture of the school and the problem of change* (Englewood Cliffs, NJ: Prentice Hall, 1971); M. Lampert, How do teachers manage to teach? Perspectives on problems in practice, *Harvard Educational Review, 55*(2), 178–194.

6. Herbert Simon coined the word "satisfice." See his *Models of Man* (New York: John Wiley Co., 1957), 204–205.

7. All names used in examples and cases are pseudonyms.

8. See Schön (1983); L. Cuban, Managing dilemmas while building professional communities, *Education Researcher, 21*(1), 4–11.

9. L. Payer, *Medicine and culture* (New York: Henry Holt and Co., 1988), 131, 137; Barzini is also quoted here.

10. G. Myrdal, *An American dilemma* (New York: Harper and Brothers, 1944).

11. This case is adapted from one that Don Hill, a veteran San Francisco Bay area social-studies teacher, created for a leadership institute held at the Professional Development Center of the Stanford/Schools Collaborative in June 1991.

12. Leithwood & Steinbach (1995), 171–194; also M. Rokeach & S. Ball-Rokeach, Stability and change in American value priorities, 1968–1981, *American Psychologist, 44*(5), 775–784.

13. J. Adams, *Conceptual blockbusting* (San Francisco: San Francisco Book Company, 1976), 15.

14. R. Edmonds, Effective Schools for the Urban Poor, *Educational Leadership, 37*(1), 15–27; S. Purkey & M. Smith, Effective schools: A review, *Elementary School Journal, 83* 427–452.

15. M. Twain, *Tom Sawyer and Huckleberry Finn* (London: Everyman's Library, 1943), 12–13.

16. L. Bolman & T. Deal, *Reframing organizations: Artistry, choice, and leadership* (San Francisco: Jossey-Bass, 1991); K. S. Louis, J. Toole, & A. Hargeaves, Rethinking school improvement, in J. Murphy & K. S. Louis (Eds.), *Handbook of research on educational administration,* 2nd ed. (San Francisco: Jossey-Bass, 1999), 251–276. D. Tyack, Ways of seeing, *Harvard Educational Review, 46*(3); B. Malen & M. Knapp, Rethinking the multiple perspectives approach to education policy analysis: Implications for policy–practice connections, *Journal of Education Policy, 12*(5), 419–445.

17. This case is drawn from my personal experience as a teacher and from the experience of three teachers I worked with in the San Francisco Bay area of Northern California. All names are pseudonyms.

18. This case comes from a principal in a Midwestern state who wrote of his experiences in this school for a workshop. I have deleted all identifying references.

19. This case is a composite of three novice teachers I have worked with in the past decade. All names are fictitious.

20. This case comes from the experiences of a Minnesota middle-school principal.

21. D. Tyack & L. Cuban, *Tinkering toward utopia* (Cambridge, MA: Harvard University Press, 1995).

22. L. Cuban, The media and polls in education over the years, in Gene Maeroff (Ed.), *Imaging education* (New York: Teachers College Press, 1998), 69–82; L. Cuban, *How teachers taught*, 2nd ed. (New York: Teachers College Press, 1993).

23. For these distinctions about change, I have drawn from my earlier work. See L. Cuban, A fundamental puzzle of school reform, *Phi Delta Kappan, 69*(5), 340–344, and L. Cuban, Reforming again, again, and again, *Educational Researcher, 19*(1), 3–13. Much of my thinking then was influenced by P. Watzlawick, R. Frisch, & J. Weakland, *Change: Principles of problem formation and problem resolution* (New York: Norton, 1974). Since then I have broadened my initial framework, which was geared to public schools in the United States, to include higher education. See L. Cuban, *How scholars trumped teachers: Change without reform in university research, curriculum, and teaching, 1890–1990* (New York: Teachers College Press, 1999). Also, I found the formulation of change offered by L. Cerych, The policy perspective, in B. Clark (Ed.), *The higher education system: Academic organization in cross-national perspective* (Berkeley: University of California Press, 1983), most helpful.

24. Cuban (1993); Cuban (1999).

25. This case comes from a principal who led this school for five years. I have added sections to fill in gaps in the administrator's description. All names are fictitious.

References

Adams, J. (1976). *Conceptual blockbusting.* San Francisco: San Francisco Book Company

Berlak, A., & Berlak, H. (1981). *Dilemmas of schooling.* London: Methuen.

Billig, M., Condor, S., Edwards, D., Gane, M., Middleton, D., & Radley, A. (1988). *Ideological dilemmas: A social psychology of everyday thinking.* Newbury Park, CA: SAGE Publications.

Bolman, L., & Deal, T. (1991). *Reframing organizations: Artistry, choice, and leadership.* San Francisco: Jossey-Bass.

Cerych, L. (1983). The policy perspective. In B. Clark (Ed.), *The higher education system: Academic organization in cross-national perspective.* Berkeley: University of California Press.

Cuban, L. (1988). A fundamental puzzle of school reform. *Phi Delta Kappan, 69*(5), 340–344.

Cuban, L. (1990). Reforming again, again, and again. *Educational Researcher, 19*(1), 3–13.

Cuban, L. (1992). Managing dilemmas while building professional communities. *Education Researcher, 21*(1), 4–11.

Cuban, L. (1993). *How teachers taught* (2nd ed.). New York: Teachers College Press.

Cuban, L. (1998). The media and polls in education over the years. In G. Maeroff (Ed.), *Imaging education.* New York: Teachers College Press.

Cuban, L. (1999). *How scholars trumped teachers: Change without reform in university research, curriculum, and teaching, 1890–1990.* New York: Teachers College Press.

Dewey, J. (1933). *How we think.* Boston: D. C. Heath.

Edmonds, R. (1979). Effective schools for the urban poor. *Educational Leadership, 37*(1), 15–27.

Elbow, P. (1983). Embracing contraries in the teaching process. *College English, 45*(4), 327–339.

Gaynor, A. (1998). *Analyzing problems in schools and school systems.* Mahwah, NJ: Lawrence Erlbaum Associates.

Getzels, J. W. (1982). The problem of the problem. In R. Hogarth (Ed.), *New directions for methodology of social and behavioral science: Question framing and response consistency* (no. 11;). San Francisco: Jossey-Bass.

Haley, J. (1976). *Problem-Solving therapy.* New York: Harper and Row.

Hayes, J. (1981). *The complete problem solver.* Philadelphia: Franklin Institute.

Kingdon, J. (1995). *Agendas, alternatives, and public policies* (2nd ed.). New York: HarperCollins College Publishers.

Lampert, M. (1985). How do teachers manage to teach? Perspectives on problems in practice. *Harvard Educational Review, 55*(2), 178–194.

Leithwood, K. & Steinbach, R. (1995). *Expert problem solving: Evidence from school and district leaders.* Albany: State University of New York Press.

Louis, K. S., Toole, J., & Hargeaves, A. (1999). Rethinking school improvement. In J. Murphy & K. S. Louis (Eds.), *Handbook of research on educational administration* (2nd ed.). San Francisco: Jossey-Bass.

Malen, B., & Knapp, M. (1997). Rethinking the multiple perspectives approach to education policy analysis: Implications for policy–practice connections. *Journal of Education Policy, 12*(5), 419–445.

Mason, R. & Mitroff, I. (1981). *Challenging strategic planning assumptions: Theory, cases, and techniques.* New York: John Wiley & Sons.

Mayer, R. (1992). *Thinking, problem solving, cognition* (2nd ed.). New York: W. H. Freeman.

Myrdal, G. (1944). *An American dilemma.* New York: Harper and Brothers.

Payer, L. (1988). *Medicine and culture.* New York: Henry Holt and Co.

Purkey, S., & Smith, M. (1983). Effective schools: A review. *Elementary School Journal, 83,* 427–452.

Rokeach, M., & Ball-Rokeach, S. (1989). Stability and change in American value priorities, 1968–1981. *American Psychologist, 44*(5), 775–784.

Sarason, S. (1971). *The culture of the school and the problem of change.* Englewood Cliffs, NJ: Prentice Hall.

Schön, D. (1983). *The Reflective practitioner: How professionals think in action.* New York: Basic Books.

Shulman, L. & Elstein, A. (1978). *Medical problem solving.* Cambridge, MA: Harvard University Press.

Simon, H. (1957). *Models of man.* New York: John Wiley Co.

Twain, M. (1943). *Tom Sawyer and Huckleberry Finn.* London: Everyman's Library.

Tyack, D. (1976). Ways of seeing. *Harvard Educational Review, 46*(3), 355–389.

Tyack, D., & Cuban, L. (1995). *Tinkering toward utopia.* Cambridge, MA: Harvard University Press.

Watzlawick, P., Frisch, R., & Weakland, J. (1974). *Change: Principles of problem formation and problem resolution.* New York: Norton.

About the Author ❖

Larry Cuban is Professor of Education at Stanford University, Stanford, California, where he teaches courses in the history of school reform, leadership, and policy analysis. He has been faculty sponsor of the Stanford/Schools Collaborative and the Stanford Teacher Education program.

Professor Cuban's background in the field of education prior to becoming a professor includes fourteen years of teaching high-school social studies in inner-city schools, administering teacher-training programs at school sites, and serving for seven years as a district superintendent.

Trained as a historian, Professor Cuban received a B.A. degree from the University of Pittsburgh in 1955 and an M.A. from Cleveland's Case Western Reserve University three years later. On completing his Ph.D. work at Stanford University in 1974, he became superintendent of the Arlington County (Virginia) public schools, a position he held until he returned to Stanford in 1981.

His major research interests focus on the history of curriculum and instruction, educational leadership, school reform, and the different versions of "good" schools, past and present. As a practitioner, he continued to work with teachers and administrators in the Stanford/Schools Collaborative and as a teacher. He has taught courses in U.S. history and economics at two different San Francisco Bay area high schools.

The author of many research and op-ed articles, Professor Cuban has written a number of books, including *Teachers and Machines: The Use of Classroom Technology Since 1920* (1986); *How Teachers Taught: Constancy and Change in American Classrooms, 1880–1990* (1993); *Tinkering Toward Utopia* (with David Tyack; 1995); *How Scholars Trumped Teachers: Change without Reform in University Curriculum, Research, and Teaching, 1890–1990* (1999); and *Reconstructing the Common Good in Education: Managing Intractable Dilemmas* (with Dorothy Shipps; 2000).